PURSUING GOD'S PRESENCE

A PRACTICAL GUIDE TO DAILY RENEWAL AND JOY

ROGER HELLAND

Chosen

a division of *Baker Publishing Group*
Minneapolis, Minnesota

© 2023 by Roger Helland

Published by Chosen Books
Minneapolis, Minnesota
www.chosenbooks.com

Chosen Books is a division of
Baker Publishing Group, Grand Rapids, Michigan

Printed in the United States of America

ISBN 978-0-8007-6327-5 (trade paper)
ISBN 978-1-4934-4109-9 (ebook)
ISBN 978-0-8007-6337-4 (casebound)

Library of Congress Cataloging-in-Publication Control Number: 2022058450

Some names and details have been changed to protect the privacy of the individuals involved.

Cover design by Darren Welch Design

Author is represented by Pape Commons

Baker Publishing Group publications use paper produced from sustainable forestry practices and post-consumer waste whenever possible.

23 24 25 26 27 28 29   7 6 5 4 3 2 1

Contents

Foreword

The great temptation of many writers and thinkers is to find a simple explanation for all the trouble we are in. We want to diagnose a root cause and then prescribe a single cure. We do this with the economy, with education, with politics, with health care and—maybe especially—with the Church. Get this wrong, we claim, and all else falls apart. Get this right, and all else comes together. Monocausal explanations are every guild's holy grail—a beautiful and valuable thing that exists, alas, solely in our imaginations.

I have read, and often been mightily persuaded by, books about the Church that purport to do just this: Posit a single cause for everything that is not working and commend a single remedy. If we only prayed more, preached better, revived our worship, reignited our evangelism, renewed our discipleship—on and on the list goes—the Church would rise up out of its stagnation and come into its flourishing.

It is a powerful vision. Too often, it is a powerful delusion.

But once in a rare while, an author happens along who nails it: He or she writes a book that traces our failures back to a single source. And then holds out the key to turning it all around.

This is that book. Dr. Roger Helland nails it. He is entirely convinced, and entirely convincing, that what ails us is one thing: we do not dwell in the presence of God—or, as he calls it, the *kāvôd* of God—God's glory. And so, the remedy is one thing: Come back. Though such a return requires resolve and discipline, it is not a tactic or a technique. It is, rather, God's immeasurable gift and beautiful invitation. It is God Himself who invites us and empowers us to share fully in His inner life. It is God Himself who desires to be with us and for us in all things and at all times.

It is God Himself who says *come*.

This insight alone is worthy of our deepest consideration. But it is what Dr. Helland does in the rest of the book that makes it so valuable: He shows us what presence-centered living looks like in virtually every realm of existence—in worship, in discipleship, in parenting, in marriage, at work and more. And then he charts a path to help get us there.

Often while reading this book, I found myself saying both *Ouch* and *Yes*. *Ouch* because, well, too often I do not dwell in God's presence. Indeed, too often I do just about everything else except that. And *Yes* because Dr. Helland's book has awakened in me a fresh desire and resolve to pursue the God who pursues me.

When I was baptized, a long time ago now, the pastor did an audacious thing: He gave me a "life verse," a passage of Scripture meant to guide me all the days of my life. It was Matthew 6:33—"But seek first the kingdom of God and his righteousness, and all these things will be added to you." That was, starting way back, God's invitation to me to pursue His presence. And I have done my level best to live by it. But sometimes I have lacked the wisdom to know how.

This book carries the explanation for what has gone wrong, and it exposes the cure for it.

Come.

Mark Buchanan, author of *God Walk: Moving at the Speed of Your Soul*; professor, Ambrose University

Acknowledgments

This is my seventh book—a labor of love to articulate the pursuit of God's presence. There are scores of people who shaped the contours of this project.

I offer my heartfelt thanks to my family, friends, colleagues and students who welcomed my ideas, and permitted me to use some of their stories. I offer special gratitude to my dear wife, Gail, who sacrificially blessed me to isolate for untold hours over the months, so I could write.

I offer a five-star commendation to the superb editorial and marketing staff of Chosen Books and Baker Publishing Group. Honorable mention goes to Kim Bangs and Stephanie Smith, and their teams, who supplied methodical expertise and a careful cover design. And Lori Janke, who supplied numerous improvements to my word-smithing and documentation.

I offer enormous gratitude to Don Pape, my agent, whose self-styled Irish tenacity and belief in me paved the way for this project. And to Mark Buchanan, whose generous foreword reflects his character and capacity as an outstanding author, and who inspires me with his availability and authenticity as a friend and colleague.

Acknowledgments

I offer a supreme salute to a cavalcade of people who directly or indirectly instructed and inspired me, ardent servants who also affirmed me and widened my ministry: Doug Balzer, Sean Campbell, Jeff Edwards, David Guretzki, Fred Hartley III, Sandy Isfeld, Cliff Jewell, Jake and Mavis Klassen, Ralph Korner, Sam Nikkel, Phil Nordin, Rob Parker, Cynthia Pelletier, John Roddam, David Ruis, Dan Slade, Phil Wagler, Kara Wilfley, and the late John Wimber.

And finally, I offer my applause to a roster of people, too many to mention, whose works or names I cite. These fellow travelers champion the journey of pursuing God's presence.

Introduction

From Pagan to Presence

People ask me, "What's your background?" My reply is always, "Pagan!" I grew up as a non-Christian in Southern California with a sin-infested lifestyle that was devoid of God. Our family never attended church, read the Bible or prayed. And Jesus Christ was a swear word. My stepdad was a realtor, and my mother was a waitress. I groped in spiritual darkness until I was nearly eighteen.

One December Friday night, while I was at home on leave from boot camp in the United States Army stationed at Fort Ord, California, a high school friend and I drove up into the foothills on Glendora Mountain Road to overlook the city. This was the place where in high school we would all land to drink and do drugs. While I was at Fort Ord, however, my friend had shockingly become a "Jesus freak." Around 10:00 p.m., while I peaked on LSD, he shared the Gospel with me. The Spirit pierced my darkness. I felt this gravitational pull—of *presence*.

11

I gazed into the winter night sky and prayed my first prayer. *"Jesus, if You're real, I want to believe."*

From Pagan to Pastor

Jesus took me up on my offer. Six weeks later, on a frigid, sun-glaring Saturday morning, I sat alone on my bunk in the barracks at Fort Lewis, Washington, my newly assigned Army base. I was reading John's gospel from a blue leather-covered King James Version Bible my stepdad had given me. An inrush of joy and impeccable light beamed into my heart and soul. As I look back, it was my personal Pentecost—of *presence*—where the Spirit saturated me. That is when I recognized I was a convert who had become a conscious follower of Jesus Christ.

It took several years for Jesus to scrub me of my pagan filth. I lived a double life with my Army buddies, though I felt the fire of my newfound faith. The tipping point came in the barracks one Saturday night in Kitzingen, West Germany, where I was later based. As I tried to talk about Jesus to a guy, he hurled an unforgettable indictment at me.

"Roger, get your story straight. You've got a beer in one hand and a Bible in the other."

Like Nathan, the prophet who confronted King David, that soldier confronted me. I pivoted, raced to my room and wept bitterly over the hypocrisy of my life. But God's convicting *presence* blanketed me. Two years later, after my military discharge, a pastor baptized my sun-tanned body and shoulder-length hair in the chilly waters of a Newport Beach, California, lagoon.

I enrolled at Mount San Antonio College in Walnut, California, to study forestry in a two-year associate of arts program. I also worked part time as a custodian in the Glendora School District. I was alone one evening midway through my second year vacuuming the carpet at the Goddard Middle School library. I stopped, turned the vacuum off and stood there motionless in the center of the room. I had that feeling you get when you think someone is watching you. I was hushed and drawn into a holy place of *presence*. Deep inside (it is hard to explain), I had this inner nudge. I felt a summons to ministry as a profession. This led to several divine appointments in which I left California and headed due north to Canada to attend a small Bible college in Surrey, British Columbia.

After Bible college, I had another nudge toward further study, and I spent four years at Dallas Theological Seminary. I acquired a passion for Bible exposition and teaching. That led to a teaching position at Okanagan Bible College in Kelowna, British Columbia. My first day on campus, two church leaders appeared at the front office to see me. They were following up on a mutual friend's referral and invited my wife and me to join them in a new church plant. That initial group of young Bible-believing Baptist and Brethren leaders eventually became New Life Vineyard Fellowship. We agreed to join. I started as an elder.

Two years in, on December 9, 1987, during a pastors, elders and wives Christmas dinner held at the home of one of the elders, I had this nudge for us to pray together. Since we were about to wrap up and leave, everyone resisted. But I persisted. Eventually, that group of eight couples consented to pray. About ten minutes later, heaven came down and glory filled our souls! We experienced a dramatic visitation of God's presence that ignited razor-sharp prophecy and repentance. This was accompanied by physical manifestations like those you read about in revivals. Four and a half hours later, around 2:30 a.m., we staggered out.

That prayer time unleashed what would become a church-wide river of renewal with local and international impact. God forever altered us. John White's book *When the Spirit Comes with Power* helped us comprehend the energies and effects of God's presence that stampede from revivals. Our vision became "More!"

Four years later, I had that same nudge to leave the Bible college and serve as the senior associate pastor of New Life, then briefly as senior pastor. That completed my journey from pagan to pastor. Like Jesus in the temple, I received a zeal for God's presence that consumed me (see John 2:17). I designed church conferences, a church-based school of ministry and an international ministry school to catalyze spiritual renewal. This inspired my first two books, *Let the River Flow* (1996) and *The Revived Church* (1998).

From Pastor to Pray-er

As I pastored, I began to view prayer as the core spiritual practice that activated and sustained spiritual and missional renewal. I noticed we could not preach physical healing into people, counsel demonic oppression away from people, program chronic sin out of people or argue the Kingdom over people. I would watch church leaders like John Wimber gently pray, "Come, Holy Spirit" and witness mind-boggling results. I would emerge from Spirit-inflamed gatherings with a high-definition awareness of God's presence, and I became power-boosted with mountain-moving faith and exhilarating freedom. I adopted James Ryle's motto for freedom that I heard him preach several years ago at a conference: "Nothing to fear, nothing to prove, nothing to hide and nothing to lose."

Then, through a series of those inner nudges during inquiring prayer, the Lord led my wife, Gail, and I to pastor in a Mennonite Brethren and a Christian and Missionary Alliance church in British Columbia. I also served as a district minister of the Baptist General Conference in Alberta.

I love the Church and various theological traditions, but I grew frustrated and dissatisfied with the Church's condition. I saw prayerless pastors and churches grind out human life and leadership. I left many church and denominational meetings that felt hollow, crowded with words, devoid of prayer and *rûah* (Hebrew for *Spirit*). Jack Deere has a point when he says, "The biggest difference between the first-century church and the modern church in the Western world is that the first-century church was a praying church. We are a talking church."[1]

The Lord hauled me into an expedition of devotion to prayer. Some guides along the way were Mike Bickle, Jim Cymbala, Daniel Henderson and Ray Duerksen. Others included E. M. Bounds, Andrew Murray, Henri Nouwen and Ruth Haley Barton. I welcomed God's invitation and impartation for devotion to prayer and the ministry of the Word (see Acts 6:4). I also obtained a passion to pray for the sick inside and outside of religious settings. It became a natural supernatural part of my ministry as a spiritual leader. I trekked from pastor to pray-er.

In the spring of 2020, near the end of thirteen years as a district minister, the Lord lodged a sentence into my mind. As I prayed one morning in my home office, He nudged, "You'll be praying for leaders." That became primer guidance for what was ahead. I was in the throes of organizing and participating in prayer gatherings for revival as Pentecost Sunday loomed in late May 2020. The Evangelical Fellowship of Canada invited me to lead four weekly one-hour Zoom prayer gatherings. We prayed for holiness, healing, the Spirit's outpouring, and revival across Canada and the nations. God's presence was palpable in those Zoom prayer times. Those prayer sessions spawned an invitation for me to join the EFC as their prayer ambassador to develop prayer with and for its affiliates and other prayer initiatives. At the heart of all this, I was resolved to seek and host God's presence—from pray-er to presence.

From Pray-er to Presence

You will discover in chapter 1 how God seized me to pursue a presence-centered life. I love the Spirit and Scripture.

Charismatics embrace a robust Spirit theology. Conservatives embrace a rich Scripture theology. Empowered evangelicals embrace both. Dallas Seminary taught me how to exegete Scripture, and the Vineyard taught me how to experience the Spirit. The Spirit partners with the Scripture like breath and voice. I consider with theology, and I cultivate with practices to explore what biblical Hebrew calls the *kāvôd* (pronounced *kaw-vode*) of God—the glory of God—His manifest presence. You may be familiar with the term *shekinah*. Its Hebrew root means "to dwell" (see Exodus 25:8). Although the Bible does not use it, rabbis have used it to identify God's localized dwelling presence—His *shekinah* glory.

To pursue God's presence, His glory, is to seek God's face and His person through prayer, awareness, surrender and obedience by Scripture-informed faith. In this New Testament age of the Spirit, God graces local churches with the manifestation—appearance—of the Spirit's presence (see 1 Corinthians 12:7). The key to fervent prayer, effective Bible study, intimate worship, anointed preaching, authentic fellowship, active churches and flourishing families is God's reverberating presence. Marvelous results occur when His localized presence moves in closer than a tight hug—holiness, healing, transformation and joy. Habakkuk 2:14 fuels my vision. "For the earth will be filled with the knowledge of the glory [*kāvôd*] of the LORD as the waters cover the sea." May you foster a firsthand, experiential, intimate knowledge of God's glory as full and vast as the sea!

Like a captivating movie, I have been on an adventure from pagan to pastor to pray-er to presence. When we meet God's *kāvôd*, nothing on earth can duplicate or replace it. We will explore how to seek, experience and host God's presence. Let Psalm 105:4 regulate your pursuit. "Seek the LORD and his strength; seek his presence continually!"

PART 1

SEEKING GOD'S PRESENCE

1

The Search That Strengthens

Pursuing God's Presence

> The sobering truth is that the greatest hindrance to the growth of Christianity in today's world is the absence of the manifest presence of God from the church.
>
> Richard Owen Roberts[1]

A few years ago, a pastor colleague invited me to speak at a renewal conference sponsored by his Baptist church. As we chatted, he painfully recalled how his drive for over twenty grinding years had been to run and grow his church, study leadership and *do* the ministry. Fatigue and frustration choked his energy, and his methods of ministry strangled and failed him. In his early fifties, he burned out while Parkinson's barged in. He descended into an abyss to navigate the "dark night of the soul" with stiff and shaking muscles. Traumatized by disappointment and despair, like a jettisoned booster rocket, this hammered pastor nearly ditched the ministry and his hope in God.

Though he exuded integrity as a faithful spiritual leader, that did not influence God's fairness calculus. Like Job, who suffered without solutions, this tenacious pastor chose to hang on and haggle with God. He evaluated his life and leadership for over a year, the landscape of which was like a tornado-torn Oklahoma town. He exampled what Rabbi Abraham Heschel observed, "Faith like Job's cannot be shaken because it is the result of having been shaken."[2]

He emerged surrendered, liberated from his old drive, resolved to seek God's presence. And invited his congregation along to pursue God's presence with him.

Friday morning, I arrived at the church to meet with him and his staff and pray for the conference. The theme was God's presence. As I entered the auditorium and stood at the rear, we began to chat. I sensed instantly God's presence. It was so strong that I whispered, "I need to sit down." I sat on a white bench in silent reverence and looked around. A holy hush permeated the auditorium. As I choked back tears, I commented, "God's presence is here." The pastor replied, "Yeah, I know. Many people say that when they come here." That sacred presence lavished the weekend conference.

The Presence-Centered Life

Here is a series of philosophical but practical questions. What is your center? Where are your priorities and practices? How do they reflect your center? What do you think a lot about? What is your focus? I do not intend to corner you, but rather to challenge you. You might announce, "God is my center!" Good start! Well, maybe. Can you be more specific? You will see what I mean.

Parents focus on their children, students on their studies, professionals on their careers, owners on their businesses and pastors on their churches. Not necessarily bad. Some people focus on their pain, their looks or their limitations, while others focus on their past, their rights or social media. Not necessarily good. Most of us focus on our jobs, lives and livelihood, and I hope our relationships with God and loved ones. Our behaviors advertise our center, and they might shift with the seasons of life.

I will ask this another way. What do you seek continually? Your answer reveals your center—your supreme search. Before my wife and I bought our current house, we diligently searched the internet for multiple listings. Like all home buyers, we had specific priorities and values in mind. Escorted by our patient realtor, we viewed over forty houses in Airdrie, a city in Alberta, Canada. We searched for three months and discovered the new home that we bought. After all that searching, the home we bought was only two blocks away from where we were renting.

Similarly, in two situations when I was unemployed for six months, I scoured the internet, contacted friends and colleagues, prayed, emailed resumes and searched for every opportunity for work that aligned with my vision. I found a job each time. These continual searches occupied our focus and fortunately ended well.

Let me suggest a supreme search that both ensures constant discoveries and strengthens you.

The Search That Strengthens

Ponder this pungent command: "Seek the Lord and his strength; seek his presence continually" (Psalm 105:4). The first Hebrew word for *seek* means "to beat a path toward, try and reach, and inquire," and the Hebrew word for *strength* means "might" or

21

"power." The second Hebrew word for *seek* means "to discover, obtain, and look for."[3]

At times we may feel like a Boston marathoner who is running the race of his life on the verge of collapse near the finish line. It is tough to go the distance as a student, as a parent, as one who is disabled or depressed, as a widow or as an employee with a stressful job. While multitudes beat a path to alcohol, shopping, counselors or pop psychology to cope with stress, the psalmist advises us to beat a path to the Lord and reach for His supernatural strength. That is what troubled David did, and it is what I try to do. He "strengthened himself in the LORD his God" (1 Samuel 30:6).

If there were an Oscar nomination for a top catastrophe in our lifetime, the COVID-19 pandemic would surely win. Millions of discouraged people suffered from isolation and loss and were seized by anxiety and fear. Companies, churches and entire countries required innovation to survive the medical, economic and social impact. Most of us felt like modern-day hermits confined to caves of home-based, online worlds forced to work our jobs, educate our children and lead our churches through Zoom and YouTube. Introverts like me felt more at home, at least temporarily, while extroverts like my wife felt more like hostages.

COVID-19 and its variants tested our centers. Did it force you, as it did me, to face your limitations and embark on a search that strengthens? "Blessed are those whose strength is in you, in whose heart are the highways to Zion" (Psalm 84:5). Here is my interpretation of that verse: Enriched with God's favor are those who find their strength in Him, whose centers are journeys to God's presence. Zion means Jerusalem, the temple site that housed God, where Jewish worshipers sought His presence. There are no spiritual supply chain issues with God.

COVID-19 not only tested my center, but it aggravated my anxiety, a lifelong battle for me. It also tested my issues of control. Can you relate? When Russia's savage attacks on Ukraine rampaged in late February 2022, the world staggered with unnerving instability and crippling inflation. It felt as if the mountains would collapse into the sea (see Psalm 46:2).

I reset my heart on a pilgrimage to His presence, and I sensed those artesian rivers of the Spirit dwelling inside me flow with the Niagara's power (see John 7:38–39). I am fortified when I surrender my insecurity and deeply draw from God. Unceasing prayer and repentance, Scripture living and the renewing of my mind, worship and the discipline of awareness are essential services for me.

Psalm 105:4 towers as a Mount Everest text. "Seek the LORD and his strength; seek his presence continually." Did you notice the sequence? Seek the Lord and His strength—in that order. Too many Christians seek God's power over God's person, His hand over His face. I follow Mike Pilavachi and Andy Croft's wisdom, "The key to living a life full of supernatural power is to understand that the power is in the presence. As we are close to Jesus so we will see him move in us and through us. The power is in the presence. And his presence is in us."[4]

In his book *Addiction and Grace*, Dr. Gerald May declares that one hundred percent of us are addicted to something. He notes that the word *addiction* comes from the French word *attaché*, which is a junior government member who is attached to an official. If we attach to something to which we cannot say no, we have created an addiction, a center. It does not matter whether it is alcohol, television, work, recreation, money, food, shopping or social media. It becomes idolatry that does not strengthen.[5]

I taught a course on spiritual formation at Alberta Bible College. When we discussed addictions, I asked the class, "Why do people who are addicted to alcohol or drugs keep going back to them when they don't satisfy?" One astute student replied, "Because they don't satisfy."

Consider the compact word *seek*. What comes to mind? If you lost your wallet or purse, laptop or smartphone, would you seek it? How would you feel? How would you focus? If you lost sight of your child in a store or at a playground, what would you experience? Would your heart pound and your mind race with panicked focus? If you incurred enormous debt or contracted an acute disease, would you seek a solution or a cure? How focused would you be? When the COVID-19 virus invaded the globe, to what extent did that drive infectious disease scientists to seek a vaccine? That which has enormous importance can fuel our all-out searches.

Is not the act of seeking a common practice in our everyday lives? And crucial in our spiritual lives? A concordance study on *seek* could incite your imagination. Ponder these samples (emphasis added):

- O God, you are my God; earnestly I *seek* you; my soul thirsts for you; my flesh faints for you, as in a dry and weary land where there is no water (Psalm 63:1).
- With my whole heart I *seek* you; let me not wander from your commandments! (Psalm 119:10).
- But *seek* first the kingdom of God and his righteousness, and all these things will be added to you (Matthew 6:33).
- And without faith it is impossible to please him, for whoever would draw near to God must believe that he exists and that he rewards those who *seek* him (Hebrews 11:6).

Did you notice the words *earnestly* and *heart* and their connection to *seek*? And God rewards those who seek Him. Compelling? There is a final Hebrew word in Psalm 105:4 to interpret for the presence-centered life. The psalmist trumpets the call to seek His presence continually. The Hebrew word often translated as *presence* is *paneh*, which means "face."[6]

In the Bible, God's face refers to His entire being as one who eyes us with full attention, in proximity with His personal and relational presence. An alternate translation would be "seek His face always"—or the paraphrase, to look for God without interruption. To seek God's face is to come before Him into full view. Peter Greig comments:

> In his great work *The Trinity*, Augustine repeatedly cites one particular verse, Psalm 105:4: "Seek his face always." The eminent historian Robert Louis Wilken says of this verse, "More than any other passage in the Bible it captures the spirit of early Christian thinking." In other words, if you want to understand how the early Church Fathers and Mothers successfully constructed a new intellectual and spiritual landscape for their age, the essence of their thinking and motivation was a perpetual search for the presence of God.[7]

Seeking God's Face

What is in a face? Consider your grandparents or parents, your children or grandchildren, your spouse or friends. My wife's face is lovely, charmed with grace and goodness. My grandchildren's faces are radiant, bursting with wonder and wildness. Some faces are stern while others are soft, some are worried while others are winsome, some are expressionless while others are expressive. What is in a face, a countenance? Is it not the person and their presence? The supreme search is to "seek his presence continually," or to "seek his face always" (1 Chronicles 16:11 NIV). To explore this more, let's review Psalm 27.

Imagine an Old Testament worshiper at the temple in Jerusalem. Listen to him shout a praise declaration, "The LORD is my light and my salvation; whom shall I fear?" (verse 1). He informs other worshipers of his prayer request. "One thing have I asked of the LORD, that I will seek after: that I may dwell in the house of the LORD all the days of my life, to gaze upon the beauty of the LORD and to inquire in his temple" (verse 4).

Back then, God's house was His temple—the place of His presence. Imagine living in God's house your entire life! Further down, the worshiper lets us in on his conversation with the Lord. "You have said, 'Seek my face.' My heart says to you, 'Your face, LORD, do I seek'" (verse 8).

Imagine you received a three-word text message from the Lord that read "Seek My face." A brief but stunning invitation! It is similar to one Jesus issued centuries later: "Come, follow me" (Luke 18:22). Picture God's face as revealed in Jesus Christ—relational and radiant. He is friendly, smiles and listens well. His eyes beam affection and attention your way. He bends down and gestures, "Seek Me, look for Me, chase Me."

When my grandchildren want me to chase them, they holler, "Papa, come get me!" They also love to play hide and seek, where we look for and find each other. When they succeed, they yell, "Found you!" The Lord invites us to seek and find Him.

The psalmist replies, "My heart says to you, 'Your face, LORD, do I seek.'" Our hearts speak from a dimension our minds cannot. What language does our heart use? Is it not the language of love and literature, of music and movies? Is it not the language Shakespeare crafted for *Romeo and Juliet*, and Ryan Gosling and Rachel McAdams acted for *The Notebook*?

The command center for a presence-centered life is the heart engaged in prayer as ongoing two-way communication and communion with God. Like using FaceTime with Him. Henri Nouwen reminds us, "The crisis of our prayer life is that our minds may be filled with ideas of God while our hearts remain far from him. Real prayer comes from the heart."[8]

In his book *Transforming Prayer*, Daniel Henderson fuels my prayer to seek God's face. Absorb his account as a young college student alone in his dorm room one Friday night.

I found myself flat on my face, pouring out my passionate gratitude and worship to the Savior who knew me, walked with me,
guided me, taught me, and loved me with a tender and attentive
heart. In those moments, the presence, provision, and power of
God in my life became real. Truly, I felt that if I had opened my
eyes, I would have been looking at the Holy One. . . . A "new
normal" had occurred and my soul was re-calibrated to move
beyond perfunctory prayer lists and to set my heart to seek His
face. . . . Once you have tasted this kind of prayer experience,
nothing else satisfies and everything else is seen in a new light.[9]

I identify with this report from my firsthand times in private
and public settings. They glow with an unmistakable holy ambiance that is impossible to counterfeit or conjure up. Throughout this book, I will share some of my God encounters. This
account describes the weight of God's manifest presence that
can settle on individuals or groups with the *kāvôd* of God.

The *Kāvôd* of God

When people ask, "What is your book about?" I reply, "It is
about what it means to pursue God's presence and experience
His *kāvôd*." After strange reactions, I explain what the Hebrew
word *kāvôd* (pronounced *kaw-vode*) means.

As I love ice cream, powder skiing and Los Angeles Dodgers
baseball, I love this word! Similar to the Hebrew word *shālôm*
(peace) it is packed with meaning no English word can fully
express. *Kāvôd* comes from *kābēd*, "to be heavy."[10] It can refer
to substantial honor or position (see Genesis 45:13), power
(see Isaiah 8:7) and wealth. So, Abraham was very "heavy,"
translated as "very rich in livestock, in silver, and in gold" (see
Genesis 13:2).

The *kāvôd* of God is the weight and density of His honor, radiance, majesty, power and presence—His *glory*. It is displayed
through brilliance, cloud and fire. The Old Testament Greek

version, the Septuagint, uses the word *doxa* (root of doxology or orthodoxy). It carries the meaning of *kāvôd* into the New Testament with *doxa*. Feel the weight of this text:

> For this light momentary affliction is preparing for us an eternal weight of glory beyond all comparison, as we look not to the things that are seen but to the things that are unseen. For the things that are seen are transient, but the things that are unseen are eternal.
>
> 2 Corinthians 4:17–18

The word *glory* appears over 350 times in the Bible. It became a way to speak of God Himself. God is present everywhere, always. His *omnipresence* is where He is distant and transcendent. Note David's sense when he asks God, "Where shall I go from your Spirit? Or where shall I flee from your presence? If I ascend to heaven, you are there! If I make my bed in Sheol [the abode of the dead], you are there!" (Psalm 139:7–8).

I showed the dusty Mars landscape to seminary students with a video panorama beamed to earth from the Perseverance rover when Mars was 130 million miles away. I also showed them the most distant galaxies ever seen—nine billion light-years away—from photos the Hubble telescope shot. I declared, "God is as present on Mars and in the distant universe as He is in your room right now!" They sat stunned. Jeremiah asks, "Can a man hide himself in secret places so that I cannot see him? declares the LORD. Do I not fill heaven and earth? declares the LORD" (Jeremiah 23:24). Baffles your mind! We are usually not conscious of His omnipresence.

There are also times when God's presence is vivid and intense—His *manifest presence*—where He is localized and immanent. We are conscious of Him and His influence. Electric times can occur, like in the *Velveteen Rabbit*. In this story, a boy so loves his stuffed rabbit that it becomes real. When God is involved, there are times in which you become real, buzzing inside, aware of God's unmistakable nearness of love and inner glow. "Once you are real you can't become unreal again. It lasts for always."[11] The weight of God's *kāvôd*, His glory, has an impact on you.

Like the surging sun, God's glory surges in His Person. Like the sun's light, God's brilliant glory is manifest or shown. God is light (see 1 John 1:5). He illuminates, warms and guides us. Jesus experienced God's eternal presence and glory. "And now, Father, glorify me in your own presence with the glory that I had with you before the world existed" (John 17:5).

We recognize the weight of presence. Extraordinary leaders such as Billy Graham, Michelle Obama, Martin Luther King Jr. or Queen Elizabeth II radiate a confident presence to millions of people through their words and personalities. You know ordinary people whose influence can stir you at times. Perhaps you have had those situations where the worship, preaching, teaching or prayer entered another dimension and became dense with awe, peacefulness, serenity, euphoria or quickening.

Whether cultivated or spontaneous, there are occasions when God makes Himself known to us in dramatic or subtle ways. Some people have physical or emotional reactions or experience healing or deliverance, filling of the Spirit, or the fear of God and repentance. At other times the effects are less detectable. I have witnessed scores of church gatherings and Zoom prayer times where the aura of God's *kāvôd* was tangible. When they were drawn into a sacred zone, people became speechless and motionless and left the meetings with an "afterglow."

In fact, a mature leader told me that even a few hours after a Zoom prayer meeting ended, he continued to weep and felt the lingering effects of the Spirit. I led a Zoom prayer gathering with over one hundred leaders for the Canadian federal election in September 2021. A woman pastor remarked in an email to me later, "I could feel the power and the Holy Spirit's presence as we were gathering and waiting for the meeting to start! Like burning coals were being heaped together, ignition and a blazing, with a passionate sense of unity and power. So good!"

The *kāvôd* of God and the face of God manifest the personal presence of God with us. What marks God's people is God's *presence*. The Bible reports how Israel so incited the Lord's wrath that He decided to inflict disaster on them (see Exodus 32). They built a golden calf idol when they grew impatient waiting for Moses to return from Mount Sinai. Moses appealed to the Lord on their behalf, and the Lord conceded.

God commanded Moses to leave Sinai but threatened not to go with His stiff-necked people. When Israel heard this disastrous word, they mourned while God decided what to do with them. Imagine the anxiety you would feel if God fumed at you, "I am not going with you!" Moses asked the Lord who He intended to send with him and this nation as His people. God softened and offered Himself. Their final conversation injects needed relief and confidence to pursue the presence-centered life.

> And he said, "My presence [face] will go with you, and I will give you rest." And he said to him, "If your presence [face] will not go with me, do not bring us up from here. For how shall it be known that I have found favor in your sight, I and your people? Is it not in your going with us, so that we are distinct, I and your people, from every other people on the face of the earth?" And the LORD said to Moses, "This very thing that you have spoken I will do, for you have found favor in my sight, and I know you by name." Moses said, "Please show me your glory [*kāvôd*]." And he said, "I will make all my goodness pass before you and will proclaim before you my name 'The LORD.'"
>
> Exodus 33:14–19

Consider the word *with*. Short and substantial. May joy rush through you as you recognize that God races down from His holy mountain to grant us His personal presence. Here is a stunning revelation: God's glory contains His dazzling goodness! God said He would make all His goodness pass before us. The Hebrew word is *tub*. It depicts unparalleled beauty, moral excellence and spectacular quality. All God is and does is supremely good (see Psalm 119:68). And may we succeed like Joseph, Moses, Joshua, Samuel, David, Jehoshaphat, John the Baptist and the men of Cyprus and Cyrene as the hand of the Lord's favor was *with*, *upon* or *on* them.

The Path and Gladness of God's Presence

There is an voracious and ever-increasing hunger and desperate need for God's manifest presence today. As we study Scripture, we have two options: We can either lower Scripture to match the level of our experience, or we can raise our experience to match the level of Scripture. Let's hear and do God's Word and not hear it only (see Luke 11:28; James 1:22). Let this energize your walk: "Blessed are those who have learned to acclaim you, who walk in the light of your presence [face], LORD. They rejoice in your name all day long; they celebrate your righteousness" (Psalm 89:15–16 NIV).

Jesus announced, "Whoever has my commandments and keeps them, he it is who loves me. And he who loves me will be loved by my Father, and I will love him and manifest myself to him" (John 14:21). The Greek word for *manifest* is *emphanisō*. It means to "make present or visible, appear, evident to experience or the senses."[12]

How would He do this? He and His Father would come to us and make their home with us (see John 14:23). I will address some thorny issues and cheer you on to pursue a presence-centered life as a hound pursues a hare.

In *Toward a Perfect Love*, fourteenth century English author Walter Hilton wrote about the mixed life of contemplation and action. He remarks:

> A hound that runs after the hare only because he sees the other hounds running will, when he grows weary, just sit down and rest or turn around and head home. But if he runs because he actually sees the hare, he will not spare himself for weariness until he has it. Whoever can most intensely desire God shall most intensely experience him.[13]

The last session of that weekend renewal conference I referred to earlier occurred on a Sunday morning. I arrived an hour early to join the pastor and the staff in his office for pre-service prayer. As we prayed, God's presence settled in as a morning fog. For about half an hour, the Spirit led our Scripture-fed prayers. I did not want to leave, but I had to. I was the speaker that morning. As I ventured into the auditorium, a familiar quality permeated the people. When several people greeted or prayed for me, I felt laser-pierced. They were hosts of God's presence. I teetered some and sat down.

An *unction* carried our worship and my message and shuddered our souls. While there, we anointed the pastor with oil and prayed God would heal him of Parkinson's disease. Unfortunately, God has not healed him yet. And two years later, to make matters worse, as he was out for a bike ride, a truck stopped to let two deer cross the road. He careened into a ditch to avoid the truck. He suffered injuries to his neck, ribs and lungs that required traction to brace him upright for several months. He recovered. He and his church are rugged presence pioneers on a mission to clear a path as a people of His presence, led by His presence.

In his Pentecost sermon, Peter cites David, who points to Jesus in Psalm 16:8–11 from the Greek Old Testament (the Septuagint). May this text point you to an unshakable life in the Lord that luxuriates in presence-centered gladness and joy:

> For David says concerning him, "I saw the Lord always before me, for he is at my right hand that I may not be shaken; therefore my heart was glad, and my tongue rejoiced; my flesh also will dwell in hope. For you will not abandon my soul to Hades, or let your Holy One see corruption. You have made known to me the paths of life; you will make me full of gladness with your presence."
>
> Acts 2:25–28

On Monday afternoon, I flew home resolved to seek God's presence. And I invite you along with me to pursue a presence-centered life.

2

From Eden to Eternity

Presence-Centered Salvation

The kind of revival we need today is a revival of reverence
and sacredness in the presence of God. This needs to happen personally and then flow over into the church setting.

A.W. Tozer[1]

What stands out to you with the Garden of Eden story in Genesis 1–3? Creation, Adam and Eve, the serpent and forbidden fruit, the Fall?

What stands out to me is God's *presence* as He strolls in His Garden of Eden in the East near the Tigris and Euphrates rivers (see Genesis 2:8, 14). God's manifest presence with us bookends the salvation story from Eden in Genesis to eternity in Revelation.

My wife, like many who have a green thumb, loves to work gardens and flower beds. I dislike gardening. I even avoid mowing the lawn! All the yardwork my parents consigned me to do as a young lad under the searing Southern California sun must have traumatized me for life. All gardens, whether they are simple gardens or lavish gardens such as Canada's Butchart Gardens, beget sore backs and soiled fingers. I avoid the Fall-imposed curse on Adam, who worked a thorns-infested ground, sweat-faced (see Genesis 3:17–19), to walk in a groomed garden on a cool day.

Here is what occurred soon after the forbidden fruit debacle with Satan. Attired in custom fig leaf garments to cover their shamed nakedness, earth's first couple "heard the sound of the LORD God walking in the garden in the cool of the day, and the man and his wife hid themselves from the presence [face] of the LORD God among the trees of the garden" (Genesis 3:8). What did they hear: rolling thunder, rustling trees or currents of evening wind? The Hebrew uses "wind [*rûah*] of the day." Tough to say. They did encounter God's manifest presence, which evoked dreadful fear.

It appears garden walks and God's presence go together.

When we stroll in parks with family or friends, we walk and talk in relationships. Physical walks can represent spiritual walks of devout people who live close to God. Enoch and Noah "walked with God" (Genesis 5:22; 6:9). Later, Micah set requirements, "to do justice, and to love kindness, and to walk humbly with your God" (Micah 6:8). And Paul exhorted, "Therefore, as you received Christ Jesus the Lord, so walk in him" (Colossians 2:6). In *God Walk*, Mark Buchanan wrote, "Walking is a primary way of knowing God."[2]

I enjoy walks with my wife, grandchildren, friends and colleagues. Walks invigorate the body and soul with brisk oxygen, sun, exercise and conversation. And walks evacuate stress. Like mothers with babies, walks can generate bonding with others. I also enjoy walks with God. I will saunter the neighborhood or a nearby park to walk and talk with Him, to pray, to occasionally pout and to practice His presence. To know God.

When God walks and talks with people, He offers His relational presence. His policy is to dwell with us. We detect a forecast for a coming tabernacle and temple—habitations of God's manifest presence—where God promises, "I will make my dwelling [tabernacle] among you. . . . And I will walk among you" (Leviticus 26:11–12). Scholars teach that Eden was a temple of God, a local dwelling place, His home where He first walked on earth. And more specifically, the holiest site had God's garden as its atrium. Scripture considers the heavens itself as the grand cosmic temple of God filled by His *kāvôd*, His glory (see Psalm 8, Isaiah 66).

John Walton comments, "When we consider the Garden of Eden in its ancient context, we find that it is more *sacred space* than *green space*. It is the center of order, not perfection, and its significance has more to do with divine presence than human paradise."[3] View the Garden as more of a lush, landscaped botanical park than a vegetable plot. Ezekiel calls Eden a temple, "the garden of God. . . . the holy mountain of God" (Ezekiel 28:13–14). Mountains and sanctuaries are both connected elsewhere to the temple and tabernacle (see Exodus 15:17; Leviticus 21:23).[4] The Hebrew word *Eden* means "delights" or "luxury."[5]

The entrance to the Garden was from the East (see Genesis 3:24) as it was to the tabernacle and temple (see Numbers 3:38; Ezekiel 47:1). The Tree of Life centered in the Garden and the river of life that flowed into it depict images of life-generating sources from God's presence that nourish His people (see Genesis 2:8–9). The temple visions in Ezekiel 47 and Revelation 22 amplify these images.

First published in 1667, blind English Puritan John Milton wrote the classic *Paradise Lost*. In it, he dramatizes Adam and Eve's Fall and their exile from Eden—paradise lost. Milton writes, "Of man's first disobedience, and the fruit of that forbidden tree, whose mortal taste brought death into the world, and all our woe."[6]

> Then the LORD God said, "Behold, the man has become like one of us in knowing good and evil. Now, lest he reach out his hand and also take of the tree of life and eat, and live forever—" therefore the LORD God sent him out from the garden of Eden to work the ground from which he was taken. He drove out the man, and at the east of the garden of Eden he placed the cherubim and a flaming sword that turned every way to guard the way to the tree of life.
>
> Genesis 3:22–24

It is difficult to fathom such a severe penalty; however, it is matched with a severe mercy. It is worse than having to "wait till your dad gets home," or having to wait in your boss's office or being required to serve time at San Quentin prison. It is worse than anything you can imagine, except for God's death penalty in which the couple "shall surely die" (Genesis 2:17).

First, there is eviction. God sent out Adam and Eve from the Garden to work a now cursed ground. God banished the couple from Eden.

Second, there is exile. God drove out Adam (*east* of the Garden) and blocked access to the Garden and the Tree of Life with cherubim and a swinging, flaming sword.

These angels appear later as gold winged ornaments facing each other on the mercy seat atop the Ark of the Covenant box in the Holy of Holies in the tabernacle and temple. When Cain murdered his brother Abel, God also evicted and exiled him from both the ground and God's face (see Genesis 4:14). So, "Cain went away from the presence [face] of the LORD and settled in the land of Nod, east of Eden" (Genesis 4:16). Earth's first family became banished fugitives.

Paradise lost—God banished and blocked humanity from His manifest presence.

From Eden to the Ends of the Earth

With its first tenants now evicted, God's luscious Garden would not be tended anymore. Slammed with God's double penalty, like wildfires that ravage California forests, spiritual and physical death ravaged Adam and Eve and every human being yet to come born in sin.

Recall what it is like when people withdraw their presence from you. If God withdraws His, now what? Good news: We are not entombed in sin and disorder from consumed fruit that would keep us alive forever. Bad news: We face both spiritual and physical death and the prospect of remaining alienated from God forever. He can no longer reside with His banished unholy people. And if God's policy is to live with His people, He is unhappy being homeless.

As I sit in my home office, the sanctuary where I do much of my work and writing, I gaze out the window at the effects of spring. At times the view is snow-covered, and at other times it is green and lush. It is the same view in winter, summer or fall. It offers a pause, a breather, a soul recharging. I view the stately trees that border our neighbor's backyard as they sway in the wind. They accentuate the sky towering above that offers gold, blue, gray or black shades depending on the type of weather and the time of day.

The view directs me to the God of Creation, redemption, grace and gardens who wants to walk and talk with me. It also reminds me that although Eden was long ago, God is working an immense plan to extend Eden to the ends of the earth. A Gospel plan. An epic narrative of paradise restored. Of God with us.

It started well. God placed royal representations of Himself—images or icons—in His temple Garden with Adam and Eve. Genesis 1:26–28 declares God made humanity in His image to have royal dominion in all the earth, to be fruitful and multiply and to fill and subdue it. Scholars teach that the Ancient Near Eastern practice was to place images or statues of a god in garden-like temples. Ancient kings would place images or statues of themselves in distant lands they ruled to represent their sovereign presence. But sin marred God's image bearers.

After the exile from Eden, the pandemic of sin coursed through humanity. God grieved about making humanity, but He also noticed righteous Noah. God issued instructions for him to build a boat that would float with the world's largest zoo aboard for five months until the flood receded. He cleansed the world of wicked people—temporarily.

Abraham arrived centuries later. God cut a covenant with him to bless the world through him and his family line. God reiterated the commission to Adam to be fruitful and fill the earth as He blessed Abraham and promised to multiply him, make him fruitful and make his descendants into nations (see Genesis 17:2, 6). God extended Eden outward.

Because of sin, a chasm developed between a holy God and His unholy people as deep and wide as the Grand Canyon. God intended, therefore, to bridge that chasm using the Old Testament tabernacle and temple. He planned to extend Eden to the ends of the earth through Jesus Christ and the Church.

Tabernacle

God did not primarily engineer the tabernacle and temple so we could approach and worship Him as a holy people. He did it so He could approach and live with us as a holy God. God's design and desire is to dwell with us—through His manifest presence. God is unhappy being homeless. When we let Him dwell with us, His presence radiates magnificent power and purity in our lives. And He initiates the home-building.

Picture Israel during their exodus from Egypt, about 600,000 men on foot, along with women, boys and girls, flocks and herds of dusty livestock (see Exodus 12:37–42). Moses led this noisy, complaining, ragtag foot parade of Hebrew refugees. God manifested His presence to guide them in a daytime pillar of cloud and a nighttime pillar of fire (see Exodus 13:21–22). Clouds and fire appear as common manifestations of God's *kāvôd* in biblical history.

Israel marched on dry ground through the walled-up Red Sea waters. They arrived and camped at Mount Sinai to hear from God through Moses and the Law that God would inscribe on stone tablets. Here they would learn how to live out their new identity as God's treasured possession, a kingdom of priests and a holy nation (see Exodus 19:1–6). Moses ascended the mountain enveloped by a cloud where the Lord's glory (*kāvôd*) dwelt as he entered God's presence. The Lord's glory (*kāvôd*) appears as a devouring fire at the mountaintop in the people's sight (see Exodus 24:15–18). Shock and awe set in!

After a forty-day mountaintop retreat with God, Moses descended with a home-building project proposal from Him. He commanded Moses to raise contributions from the people to fund it (see Exodus 25:1–7). God said, "And let them make me a sanctuary, that I may dwell in their midst. Exactly as I show you concerning the pattern of the tabernacle, and of all its furniture, so you shall make it" (Exodus 25:8–9).

It became a portable, mobile tent, called the tent of meeting, designed to temporarily house God's presence and serve as a location where He could meet with Moses and His people. God's vision was to dwell among His people whom He brought out of Egypt and be their God (see Exodus 29:45–46).

God issued detailed instructions to Moses for its construction, as well as those for the priest's clothing and consecration. If God enlisted you to build a sizable tent complex to house Him and adorn His priests in elaborate gowns and headdresses, how would you feel? After several intervening incidents, Moses erects the tabernacle, and here comes God—the climax of Exodus.

Then the cloud covered the tent of meeting, and the glory [*kāvôd*] of the LORD filled the tabernacle. And Moses was not able to enter the tent of meeting because the cloud settled on it, and the glory [*kāvôd*] of the LORD filled the tabernacle. Throughout all their journeys, whenever the cloud was taken up from over the tabernacle, the people of Israel would set out. But if the cloud was not taken up, then they did not set out till the day that it was taken up. For the cloud of the LORD was on the tabernacle by day, and fire was in it by night, in the sight of all the house of Israel throughout all their journeys.

Exodus 40:34–38

Imagine God's *kāvôd* camping out with you!

When our kids were little, we went camping. The enchantment of outdoor respite—energized by trees and thickets, sun and sand, Frisbees and firesides—drew our family together. We hiked, biked, swam and munched s'mores together. We owned a spacious two-room tent that we pitched by lakes or rivers, on grass or ground. Packed with sleeping bags, clothes, toys, food and the odd mosquito, we dwelt in that tent—especially for midday naps, rainy days and bedtime stories.

Daily at dawn, I slumped outside in a lawn chair with a Bible and a book. I would read, pray and ponder. Like parched desert sand that soaks in the rain, I soaked in the silence and solitude. I also consumed dark roast java that warmed both stomach and soul. God's presence walked my way. But we had to pack up and leave it all for home. As the kids got older, we chose more comfort and ease with cabins and cabanas. We do not camp anymore. It served a proper but temporary function. We prefer fixed cabins or cottages now. God determined camping with His people in His tent of meeting was proper, but temporary, too.

Temple

Then Samuel the prophet arrived, followed by Saul. Israel's first and tragically faulty king. But God had David, the shepherd boy, on His radar to anoint as king with whom He made an eternal covenant (see 2 Samuel 7). David informed the prophet Nathan that while he dwelt in a house of cedar, God camped in His portable tent (see verses 2–3). God was happy, though, to live in a tent during the period of the Judges (see verses 4–8). Now centuries after Moses, God decided to settle into a fixed home—the temple, the house of the Lord (see 1 Chronicles 22:1)—in Jerusalem, the capital city, to dwell with His people as part of His covenant with David. David charged his soon-to-be-king son Solomon to build a house for the Lord (see 1 Chronicles 22:6–19).

Now the climax barrels in. After seven years of meticulous construction, Solomon completed his crowning achievement. On his knees with outstretched hands, he geysers an expansive prayer of dedication to God (see 2 Chronicles 6:12–42). And then this:

> As soon as Solomon finished his prayer, fire came down from heaven and consumed the burnt offering and the sacrifices, and the glory [*kāvôd*] of the Lord filled the temple. And the priests could not enter the house of the Lord, because the glory [*kāvôd*] of the Lord filled the Lord's house. When all the people of Israel saw the fire come down and the glory [*kāvôd*] of the Lord on the temple, they bowed down with their faces to the ground on the pavement and worshiped and gave thanks to the Lord, saying, "For he is good, for his steadfast love endures forever."
>
> 2 Chronicles 7:1–3; see also 2 Chronicles 5:13–14

I have encountered God's fire in prayer with others. When that has happened, my heart, mind and body sometimes burned. There have been times when I have literally perspired. God encountered me at the Brownsville Assembly revival meetings in Pensacola, Florida, when Stephen Hill preached. He also encountered me in dozens of prayer and church meetings over the years. The flame of God's *kāvôd* furnaced my soul, where my face met the carpet prostrate in repentance. Writes Fred A. Hartley, "When God reveals himself in the fire of His tangible presence, the automatic response is to fall face down in worship. . . . When you begin to encounter the blazing fire of God's manifest presence, the fear of God is unavoidable."[7]

Fire depicts God's manifest presence. Moses, David, Solomon, Israel, Isaiah, the early Church and John met God who "is a consuming fire" (Hebrews 12:29). In the Los Angeles Azusa Street Revival of 1906–1909, sightings of fire around the building prompted calls to dispatch firemen. In 1965, a similar incident occurred during prayer at Maranatha Church in the Indonesian revival. Evan Roberts, the Welsh revival leader, called it "the divine fire."[8]

My wife and I viewed an inspiring Easter musical presentation, *Easter at the Shining Rose*, by worship artist Brian Doerksen and friends. God's presence filled our living room as I absorbed the songs from these humble musicians. Brian sang one of his classics, "Light the Fire Again." It drew me to tears. I listened and prayed my heart would not grow cold and God would light the fire again. My heart burned.

As a holy nation and royal priesthood, Israel was to mediate and display the fire of God's presence throughout the world. His glory, law and kingship would beam from the temple, where the Lord reigns (see Psalm 93–100). I love the imagery of God's idealized end-times temple that positions His mountain house as the place from which His Word goes out and the world's worship comes in (see Isaiah 2:1–5; Micah 4:1–5). But God had another temple in mind.

In 586 B.C., the Babylonians conquered the southern kingdom and destroyed Solomon's temple. Nehemiah rebuilt a mini version in 516 B.C. that King Herod expanded significantly in 20 B.C. The Western Wall in Jerusalem is all that remains of that Second Temple familiar to Jesus and the early Church the Romans destroyed, in 70 A.D. God's glory never returned to the Second Temple nor came to Herod's. His glory returned in Jesus, birthed by Mary, as God's incarnate temple.

Jesus

Why do Matthew and Luke include lengthy genealogies in their gospels? Why all those names? Like Ancestor.com, they trace the lineage of Jesus to-prove He qualifies as Israel's long-awaited and prophesied Messiah. Matthew starts with "The book of the genealogy of Jesus Christ, the son of David, the son of Abraham" (Matthew 1:1). Luke includes both David and Abraham but ends with Jesus as "the son of Adam, the son of God" (Luke 3:38). These genealogies offer a panorama of salvation history that begins with Adam in the Garden of Eden, through the promised line of blessing with Abraham and through the royal line of kingship with David. That line heads to the Garden of Gethsemane and Golgotha with Jesus.

John omits a genealogy and offers theology. "The Word became flesh and dwelt among us, and we have seen his glory, glory as of the only Son from the Father, full of grace and truth" (John 1:14). Literally, "The Word became human and tabernacled among us, and we have seen His glory . . . from the Father" (the Old Testament *kāvôd* of God). Jesus became the God-man who tented with us. Just as God's glory filled the tabernacle and later the temple, so God's glory tabernacled in Jesus and filled Him with grace and truth. God's manifest presence housed in the holy of holies now broke out into the world housed in the incarnate Son of God.

Picture Jesus early in His ministry at the annual Passover festival. He saunters up to Herod's temple in Jerusalem (see John 2:13–17). It is a flea market, a house of trade rather than a house of prayer, and Jesus rages. After He whips the merchants and animals from the temple site, the Jews whack Him with a request to justify His actions with a sign. Jesus, being both prophetic and problematic retorts, "'Destroy this temple, and in three days I will raise it up.' The Jews then said, 'It has taken forty-six years to build this temple, and will you raise it up in three days?' But He was speaking about the temple of his body" (John 2:19–21).

Jesus forecasts His death and resurrection and the destruction of Herod's temple to come in 70 A.D. By the time John wrote his gospel, the temple was gone. Jesus' physical body became God's temple to house His manifest presence. Jesus solved God's homelessness. The worship center relocated from Jerusalem to Jesus. Remember, God does not want us to live alone. He would rather live with us.

One more comment about Jesus. We read and sing about it during Christmas and watch our children dress up in robes in church plays about it. Matthew refers to it from Isaiah 7:14: "'Behold, the virgin shall conceive and bear a son, and they shall call his name Immanuel' (which means, God with us)" (Matthew 1:23). This name of Jesus is packed with presence. As I drive my Honda CRV, I will crank up the volume of a worship song by Hebrew Christian Joshua Aaron he recorded from a live concert at the Tower of David in Jerusalem. It is called "Immanuel."[9] It celebrates the truth that Jesus made His home among us and brings us face to face.

Church

God sent a duplicate copy of Himself, a human icon or image, with Jewish Jesus the Nazarene (see Colossians 1:15–17). He became a blue-collar Spirit-empowered thirty-year-old rural Savior to tabernacle among us. If He had stayed in Jerusalem after His resurrection, like Muslims who face east to pray and make pilgrimages to Mecca, we Christians would want to face Israel to pray and make pilgrimages to Jesus. Imagine the armada of jam-packed jumbo jets, cruise ships, buses and pilgrimages to the Holy Land to see and worship Jesus, the living temple of God. But God looked beyond that quandary. Rather than us going to Jesus, Jesus comes to us—by the Spirit. Different place but same presence. You will recall after the ascension of Jesus, during the Feast of Pentecost in Jerusalem fifty days later, Jesus sent the promised last days outpouring of the Holy Spirit upon 120 praying followers (see Acts 1:14–2:1–4).

Tongues of fire appeared and rested on them, and the Holy Spirit filled them. The Church became God's living temple. Jesus, who became the chief cornerstone of God's construction project, is building a universal prophetic spiritual house. It is a holy and royal priesthood, a holy nation of sons and daughters, young and old, men and women servants—the Church (see 1 Peter 2:4–10; Acts 2:1–35).

> So then you are no longer strangers and aliens, but you are fellow citizens with the saints and members of the household of God, built on the foundation of the apostles and prophets, Christ Jesus himself being the cornerstone, in whom the whole structure, being joined together, grows into a holy temple in the Lord. In him you also are being built together into a dwelling place for God by the Spirit.
>
> Ephesians 2:19–22

Christians are a people of the presence. Walking, talking temples, both gathered and scattered, houses of prayer for all the nations (see Mark 11:17). It is better Jesus left the planet early and returned to heaven ,where He could rule as the head of His Body, the Church. He promised, "It is to your advantage that I go away, for if I do not go away, the Helper [Holy Spirit] will not come to you. But if I go, I will send him to you" (John 16:7).

Paul asks, "Do you not know that you are God's temple and that God's Spirit dwells in you?" (1 Corinthians 3:16). As Jennifer Eivaz writes, we are "glory carriers"[10]—portable sanctuaries of the Spirit of glory and of God who rests upon us (see 1 Peter 4:14). Jesus deploys us to extend and mediate God's presence as His temples, to be fruitful and multiply as God's renewed images and to have dominion in Christ, from Eden to the ends of the earth (Colossians 1:5–6; 3:10). Jesus is with us for Christmas and also for the Great Commission as we make disciples. He promises, "And behold, I am with you always, to the end of the age" (Matthew 28:20). Dear reader, Jesus is *in* you and *with* you. You are safe in His embrace.

Eternity

There is a common Christian idea that believers will *go to* heaven and be with Jesus forever when they die. Instead, heaven will *come to* earth in Jesus and be with us forever. As the new Jerusalem, heaven itself descends and becomes one colossal temple that houses God's glory—His presence—as He dwells with His people. Ezekiel 40–48 informs much of the city's design and features, and Isaiah 65:17–18 provides a backdrop for a new cosmos and Jerusalem.

> Then I saw a new heaven and a new earth, for the first heaven and the first earth had passed away, and the sea was no more. And I saw the holy city, new Jerusalem, coming down out of heaven from God, prepared as a bride adorned for her husband. And I heard a loud voice from the throne saying, "Behold, the dwelling place of God is with man. He will dwell with them, and they will be his people, and God himself will be with them as their God." . . . And I saw no temple in the city, for its temple is the Lord God the Almighty and the Lamb. And the city has no need of sun or moon to shine on it, for the glory of God gives it light, and its lamp is the Lamb.
>
> Revelation 21:1–3, 22–23

The river of life flows from God's throne lined by the trees of life to invigorate the garden-like city.

Then the angel showed me the river of the water of life, bright as crystal, flowing from the throne of God and of the Lamb through the middle of the street of the city; also, on either side of the river, the tree of life with its twelve kinds of fruit, yielding its fruit each month. The leaves of the tree were for the healing of the nations.

Revelation 22:1–2

We have come full circle. Genesis 1–3 and Revelation 21–22 serve as bookends for salvation history. They demonstrate that God views the end at the beginning to dwell with His people by His manifest presence, *kāvôd*, from Eden to eternity.

3

The Pursuit of Holiness

Presence-Centered Piety

Everyone now endeavors to be eminent and distinguished
in the world, but no one is willing to learn to be pious.

Johann Arndt[1]

A few years ago, I attended a Sunday worship service that altered
the trajectory of my life. God's presence was palpable. Like a
summer breeze fragranced by a forest of ponderosa pines, a sacred ambiance blew through the worship, prayer and preaching.
It duplicated Psalm 96:9, "Worship the LORD in the splendor of
holiness; tremble before him, all the earth!" Holiness adorned
the worship. My insides trembled, especially as the sermon pa-
raded into my soul.

That Sunday morning, I suppose God instigated an encounter of His holiness with the Spirit to match an exposition of

49

His holiness with the Scripture. The pastor preached on God's meeting with Moses at the burning bush near Mount Sinai or Horeb in Exodus 3. The Lord appeared through a burning thorn bush to address eighty-year-old Moses. Never doubt God can activate senior citizens to accomplish mighty exploits for Him. Maybe Moses thought he would retire as a wilderness-worn shepherd who had tended his father-in-law Jethro's flocks.

The I AM—ever-present Lord—remembered the promise He had made with the patriarchs four centuries earlier. Now the time came to liberate His people from Egypt. He appeared to Moses in a bush that flamed with His presence but was not consumed. God's fire did not need fuel. And God never squanders His words. They altered the course of Moses' life and Israel's destiny. This sermon text seized my attention like a vice grip.

> Then he [God] said, "Do not come near; take your sandals off your feet, for the place on which you are standing is holy ground." And he said, "I am the God of your father, the God of Abraham, the God of Isaac, and the God of Jacob." And Moses hid his face, for he was afraid to look at God.
>
> Exodus 3:5–6

The active force of this Scripture pierced my soul. God roused me to pursue holiness. Whatever space God's presence or *kāvôd* occupies becomes holy. When we consider holiness, *purity* normally comes to mind. But first connect holiness with *proximity* to God's presence. To pursue God's presence demands we pursue His holiness. Duvall and Hays state:

> Wherever God's presence arrives, that space becomes holy. . . . In this regard, Exodus further develops an important theme regarding God's presence. As God becomes immanent (up close in this world), he remains totally holy. Indeed, his glory and his holiness constitute a danger and hindrance to people who desire to approach him.[2]

50

God designed the tabernacle and temple for Him to dwell in so He could walk with His people. This created a challenge. God's *kāvôd* emits unimaginable divine radiation that would dramatically affect, or should I say destroy, His unholy people with the solar winds of His consuming fire! Isaiah asks, "'Who among us can dwell with the consuming fire? Who among us can dwell with everlasting burnings?' He who walks righteously and speaks uprightly" (Isaiah 33:14–15). Blazing holiness must occupy both our walk and our talk to dwell with God.

When the worship service ended, I hightailed it to the front to receive a prayer of consecration and of impartation to pursue holiness. I nearly removed my shoes as I knew this was a sacred moment of encounter, of transformation. Bill Johnson remarks, "Face to face encounters with God often look very different from each other. . . . Such experiences have one thing in common—they make it nearly impossible for people to live as they did before they had them."[3] The pastor prayed for me, and I prayed for him. As we prayed, God's presence surged between us like a magnetic field. We had to sit down to continue our Spirit-endowed prayer. I left staggered from divine impact.

The Pursuit of Holiness and God's Presence

I have always embraced scriptural holiness as part of my spiritual upkeep—sanctification. Now I pursue it. The Holy Spirit progressively sets us apart as saints and transforms us into Christ's image. The North-Star command is "Pursue peace with all people, and holiness, without which no one will see the Lord" (Hebrews 12:14 NKJV). One present tense verb, *pursue*, governs both objects. Like the hound after the hare, it means to continually strive for or chase after peace and holiness simultaneously. If I lack peace with people, if I harbor barriers or if I am combative, I lack social holiness and I blind myself to God.

Purity enhances perception. "Blessed are the pure in heart, for they shall see God" (Matthew 5:8). Why is there not more teaching on sanctification in churches? And why is not the pursuit of holiness a compelling vision that fuels Christian life and leadership and is required for church membership? Since the word *holy* appears over six hundred times in the Bible and over seven hundred times with its derivatives *holiness, sanctification* and *sanctify*, why is it not preached more? I am astounded at how many Christians live untransformed lives.

How did mega-church pastors Bill Hybels, Carl Lentz and Bruxy Cavey start well and build global platforms only to flame out? I am wary of unaccountable, personality-driven leaders whose charisma overshadows character and whose persuasion overshadows presence. We can all traffic in truth without holiness. Scottish minister Robert Murray M'Cheyne often prayed, "Lord, make me as holy as a pardoned sinner can be made."[4]

Evidently God answered his prayer. It was reported he was so holy people wept at the very sight of him in the pulpit or when he walked down the church corridors. John Wesley warned, "The neglect of prayer is a grand hindrance to holiness."[5]

Holiness is the goal of salvation. Paul trumpets:

Blessed be the God and Father of our Lord Jesus Christ, who has blessed us in Christ with every spiritual blessing in the heavenly places, even as he chose us in him before the foundation of the world, that we should be holy and blameless before him.

Ephesians 1:3–4

God saves us so we become saints who He sets apart and destines for holiness. And Jesus urges us to "be perfect, as your heavenly Father is perfect" (Matthew 5:48). The word for *perfect* is *teleios*. It refers to a wholeness and maturity from having attained an end (*telos*). Anything is perfect when it attains the end for which it is designed.

If we marvel at the stately Tower Bridge in London, the stellar performance of a Ram 1500 pickup truck, or the beauty of Celine Dion's voice and exclaim that it is perfect, we capture the meaning of *teleios*. When we live according to God's design for us in holiness, we are perfect, true to form and aim.

I refer you to a forgotten pioneer of holiness, Phoebe Palmer (1807–1874)—a Methodist revivalist preacher from New York City considered the "mother of the holiness movement" in the nineteenth century. She was a towering renewal leader in her day. For fifty years, she held Tuesday meetings for the promotion of holiness that underscored a surrender to Christ's lordship and the cleansing baptism of the Spirit. She spoke at over three hundred camp meetings in the USA, Canada and England, and she brought 25,000 people to faith in Christ. Her impact inspired the formation of the Salvation Army, the Church of the Nazarene, the Church of God, social reform and women's ministry. She believed holiness was power and the key to revival. She also believed we must surrender to God, even when we feel nothing—emotional experiences do not confirm our faith. I agree. Instead, she held to a naked faith in the naked Word of God.

She developed an altar theology and taught that we attain holiness through three decisive and progressive steps:

1. *Consecration*. We dedicate and offer our entire self as a gift to God on the altar of Christ as a living sacrifice. He sanctifies that gift.
2. *Faith*. We believe God's Bible promises.
3. *Testimony*. We tell others about it.

Key texts for her altar theology are Hebrews 12:14, 13:10; Exodus 29:36–37; Leviticus 6:25; Matthew 23:19; and Romans 10:9–10. The way of holiness is to keep everything on the altar. Elaine Heath writes:

Palmer understands human holiness to be the experience of entire devotion to God, of being a living sacrifice on the altar of Christ, of being continuously "washed, cleansed, and renewed after the image of God" as one is ceaselessly presented to God. Romans 12:1–2 is a critical text for Palmer and the process of sanctification.[6]

Phoebe Palmer incites me to pursue holiness. She inspires me to dedicate my body, soul, spirit, time, talents and estate on the altar of Christ with a pure love of God and neighbor. Wesleyans call this *entire sanctification*. She wrote two books I found riveting: *The Way of Holiness* (1849) and *Entire Devotion to God* (1845). She pursued holiness and the *kāvôd* of God.

Holiness and the Kāvôd of God

With the word *holy*, what comes to mind? Maybe strict "pure-itans" (not Puritans) who regulate holiness from a list of dos and don'ts, rituals and rules, as the Pharisees did, designed to fortress you from the world and prevent contamination? Does it bring to mind monks, clergy, Catholic saints or people referred to as "your holiness"? Church history documents holiness movements that started with genuine Spirit fires of sanctification but ended as train wrecks of legalism or moralism. One pastor said to me, "My denomination, which began in the 19th century holiness movement, desperately needs holiness today!" Have you heard of holy children, youth, or adults who demonstrate purified and power-packed lives from God's presence? That is what Jesus has in mind for us as His holy priesthood (see 1 Peter 2:5).

Holiness is Christlikeness that gleams in our character through daily surrender. Holiness is elegant, bursting with beauty, like a dignified queen who graces a palace with class and charm. It is like a sun-drenched meadow clothed with wild-flowers in Yosemite National Park. It is like a bride who makes her way down the aisle adorned in her laced, white wedding gown and veil. Holiness adorns God's house (see Psalm 93:5). That which is separate, transcendent, radiant and pure barely captures its meaning.

Holiness beams God's magnificent perfection, His numinous presence. It implies devotion to God, piety and godliness. Holiness is relational as "God is love, and whoever abides in love abides in God, and God abides in him" (1 John 4:16). Love promotes the well-being of others. Holiness depicts wholeness and walking in love (see Ephesians 5:2). *Spirit*-ual formation is social as we respond to the Spirit's grace—for the sake of others.

Ponder Isaiah's colossal vision where he saw the Lord sitting on a throne with the flying seraphim calling back and forth to one another, "Holy, holy, holy is the Lord of hosts; the whole earth is full of his glory *kāvôd*]" [(Isaiah 6:3). Holiness emanates from God's *kāvôd*. Undone by his vision of the heavenly King, Isaiah confesses he and his people (Israel) have unclean lips. The mouth reveals a corrupt heart exposed by a holy God. A seraph then touched Isaiah's lips with a burning coal from the altar to remove his guilt and atone for his sin (see verses 6–7). I rub my lips as I pray God would cauterize my speech with winsome words purified with a holy heart.

Practical Holiness

Holiness can appear otherworldly, like Gothic cathedrals, paintings of Jesus with a halo or religious folk who say "thee" and "thou." But as God designed eagles to soar and gazelles to leap, He created us for holiness. Immorality and sexual sin are universal moral cancers that crash a wrecking ball into our design.

As a California pagan, I ran slipshod in perversion. The dark side imprisoned me. But I am now liberated in the light. Though I am one mouse click away from saucy websites, I do not venture! The internet, television, movies and celebrity culture hurl a barrage of assaults that entice moral defections from us. Our smartphones and computers have 24/7 unrestricted access to a blitzkrieg of online formation. Practical holiness is counter-formational.

I can no longer live as I once did because I am no longer the person I once was.

Paul sharply contrasts the flesh and the Spirit. "For those who live according to the flesh set their minds on the things of the flesh, but those who live according to the Spirit set their minds on the things of the Spirit" (Romans 8:5). The flesh is the fallen human condition with sinful impulses whose mind is death and hostile to God. The mind set on the Spirit is life and peace (see Romans 8:6–7).

Your mindset matters. It clenches images that color your soul. Marcus Aurelius taught, "The things you think about determine the quality of your mind. Your soul takes on the color of your thoughts."[7] Cognitive theorists report we generate about sixty thousand thoughts per day, or a thought every 1.44 seconds. We become what we think. Consider this:

> The average American adult watches TV or videos online about five to six hours a day; the average millennial is on her phone up to four hours a day. That adds up to almost a decade of your life. Barna's recent research on millennials found they spend almost 2,800 hours a year consuming digital content, but only 153 hours of that is Christ-based content; the rest is an internet cornucopia of YouTube, Instagram, Netflix, Apple, etc.[8]

What do we fill our minds with? What we view, read and hear molds our minds. Social media shapes our souls. The brain has over 200 billion neurons that compose a series of electrical highways interconnected by synapses. Those we habitually travel on become stronger. Let's "take every thought captive and make it obedient to Christ" (2 Corinthians 10:5). And "Don't copy the behavior and customs of this world, but let God transform you into a new person by changing the way you think" (Romans 12:2 NLT). Saturate in and think Spirit and Scripture.

Young adults are prone to common-law relationships, sleeping around and pornography. At pandemic levels. Like Joseph, whom Potiphar's wife tried to seduce, should we not choose to race out of the house (see Genesis 39:12)? When I was a young adult, immorality enticed me. But God wills sexual holiness. This morning I read of David's adultery with Bathsheba (see 2 Samuel 11:1–5). A lingering peek or a lustful desire can ambush us in unguarded moments. Paul teaches:

> For this is the will of God, your sanctification: that you abstain from sexual immorality; that each one of you know how to control his own body in holiness and honor. . . . For God has not called us for impurity, but in holiness. Therefore whoever disregards this, disregards not man but God, who gives his Holy Spirit to you.
>
> 1 Thessalonians 4:3–4, 7–8

Peter echoes Leviticus 19:2 and 20:7 and targets our ignorant pre-Christian character. "As obedient children, do not be conformed to the passions of your former ignorance, but as he who called you is holy, you also be holy in all your conduct, since it is written, 'You shall be holy, for I am holy'" (1 Peter 1:14–16). As children are to obey and imitate their parents, we are to obey and imitate God and bear His family likeness in holy character and conduct. The root of *holy* is *separate*, beyond the common, set apart, consecrated for God's use.

Do not let *Game of Thrones*-type dark passions mold you. Let the sunrise of godly virtue radiate through your conduct and conversation at home and at work. Pastors should consider Richard Lovelace's advice, "The minister aiming at renewal must

work toward one in which the members are growing in sanctification and making progress at conquering sin in their lives."[9]

I regularly take lethal action with the following list of earthly
evil to mortify—put to death, exterminate, banish—from my
emotions, body, mind and mouth.

> Put to death, therefore, what is earthly in you: sexual immoral-
> ity, impurity, passion, evil desire, and covetousness, which is
> idolatry. On account of these, the wrath of God is coming. In
> these, you too once walked when you were living in them. But
> now, you must put them all away: anger, wrath, malice, slander,
> and obscene talk from your mouth. Do not lie to one another,
> seeing that you have put off the old self with its practices and
> have put on the new self, which is being renewed in knowledge
> after the image of its creator.
>
> Colossians 3:5–10

Anger, wrath and malice are deadly spiritual poisons. Absorb
this stare-you-down warning. "'In your anger do not sin': Do
not let the sun go down while you are still angry, and do not give
the devil a foothold" (Ephesians 4:26–27 NIV). The Greek word
for foothold is *topos*, also translated as "place or opportunity."[10]

It is the root for the word *topography*. Satan can occupy the
topography of our lives through anger, and in doing so, gain a
spiritual stronghold. I was an angry young man who staged an
inner coup against my stepdad and the world. My wife forced
me to forgive, and as the Eagles sang, "Get over it!" I did and
reclaimed the devil's territory.

We can only kill our earthly deeds by the Spirit. "If by the
Spirit you put to death the deeds of the body, you will live" (Romans 8:13). The present tense verb suggests continuous action—
keep on putting to death bodily deeds.

In sanctification, we put off filthy rags and earthly practices
and put on new clothes. Don't you love the look and feel of new

clothes? God selects a new wardrobe that, as renewed people, we can wear—Christian clothes! These garments are five dazzling virtues we put on in contrast to the black vices we put off (see Colossians 3:8–9). Paul wheels in this rack of Christian clothing:

> Therefore, as God's chosen people, holy and dearly loved, clothe yourselves with compassion, kindness, humility, gentleness and patience. Bear with each other and forgive one another if any of you has a grievance against someone. Forgive as the Lord forgave you. And over all these virtues put on love, which binds them all together in perfect unity.
>
> Colossians 3:12–14 NIV

John Wesley taught there is no personal holiness without social holiness—how we treat others. Immorality injures others. The relational virtues of compassion, kindness, humility, gentleness and patience are for the sake of others. Holiness is relational. It is social hygiene. If I am rough, unkind or impatient, I fail to practice social holiness. And love is the outer garment that covers these five virtues in perfect unity.

A source for growth in holiness is Rob Reimer's *Soul Care*. As damaged people in body, soul and spirit, we need Jesus' power to heal the deepest parts of who we are. If we do not confess and work through sinful patterns, we crowd God out and injure others. Holiness is best forged in community, where we meet God's presence through others in grace environments. Also, consult *Life Action* Revival Worksheets[11] and Charity Gayle for worship-inspired holiness.[12]

Humility is the fount of all virtues and the doorway into holiness. In *Saint Benedict's Rule*, he offers twelve practices to ascend the degrees of humility. He states, "The first degree of humility, then, is a man always have the fear of God before his eyes."[13]

The Fear of God

When I was young, I had no fear. I toyed with firecrackers and cherry bombs. I built a hut made of tumbleweeds with a friend, and we lit a fire inside while we huddled around it on a windy night. I surfed mountain-sized waves. I motorcycled Southern California freeways helmetless on a Honda. I consumed stockpiles of mind-bending drugs and alcohol, and I cruised around intoxicated in my car with friends. Cats have nine lives, but God gave me ten despite my reckless foolishness. Worse yet is I had "no fear of God before [my] eyes" (Psalm 36:1).

As I set sail, older and wiser, to explore the limitless Atlantic of holiness, God blew 2 Corinthians 7:1 my way: "Since we have these promises, beloved, let us cleanse ourselves from every defilement of body and spirit, bringing holiness to completion in the fear of God." The context is the issue Paul raises about God's temple engaging in a consensual association with idols against Old Testament promises.

> What agreement has the temple of God with idols? For we are the temple of the living God; as God said, "I will make my dwelling among them and walk among them, and I will be their God, and they shall be my people. Therefore go out from their midst, and be separate from them, says the Lord, and touch no unclean thing; then I will welcome you, and I will be a father to you, and you shall be sons and daughters to me, says the Lord Almighty."
>
> 2 Corinthians 6:16–18

When God dwells and walks among His children, He expects us to separate ourselves from consensual idolatry that pollutes His sacred space. Timothy Keller defines an idol as "anything more important to you than God, anything that absorbs your heart and imagination more than God, anything you seek to give you what only God can give . . . a God alternative, a counterfeit

God."[14] Idols are disordered loves. Who or what controls us and sits on the throne of our hearts? Just as Paul saw in Athens (see Acts 17:16), our culture is full of idols first erected in our hearts (see Ezekiel 14:3). Sensuality, career, money, alcoholism, romance, workaholism, control, power, success, sports, self-improvement, social media and greed can rule our hearts as idols (see Colossians 3:5). If you pay attention to your irritations, they might reveal your idols.

To pursue God's presence requires purity of body and spirit. Like fornicating with a prostitute, idolatry contaminates our internal and external life (see 2 Corinthians 6:15–18).

The ritual practice to cleanse our living temples from an unholy alliance with idolatry is the fear of God. To fear God is the beginning (or head) of wisdom and our whole duty (see Proverbs 9:10, Ecclesiastes 12:13). It gushes as a fountain of life (see Proverbs 14:27). With the Spirit of the Lord resting on Him (see Isaiah 11:2), it delighted the Messiah and should delight us. "And his delight shall be in the fear of the Lord" (Isaiah 11:3). The Hebrew for *delight* is to "smell a pleasing aroma."[15]

To fear God is a posture of fragrant reverence, respect and piety, mingled with dread, awe and adoration that leads to obedience, worship and service. I have gazed across the mile-deep and eighteen miles wide Grand Canyon, peered into the universe's measureless expanse of one hundred billion galaxies, beheld the Pacific Ocean's depths that smother mountain ranges, and witnessed colossal prairie lightning storms. I retreated into a hushed dread, stricken with the fear of God. My heart leaps when I read about Job, "that there is none like him on the earth, a blameless and upright man, who fears God and turns away from evil" (Job 1:8). To fortify your fear of God, read Psalm 112.

A robust fear of God is often absent in church gatherings. And yet, here is a stark report of early Church life and growth: "Then the church throughout Judea, Galilee and Samaria enjoyed a time of peace and was strengthened. Living in the fear of the Lord and encouraged by the Holy Spirit, it increased in numbers" (Acts 9:31 NIV).

The current vision for revival draws me, but not if it is simply about more power, hype or "scarismania." The following blasts like a foghorn: "Since we are receiving a Kingdom that is unshakable, let us be thankful and please God by worshiping him with holy fear and awe. For our God is a devouring fire" (Hebrews 12:28–29 NLT).

The Pursuit of Piety and God's Presence

I am a Pietist, and in my book *The Devout Life*, I explore and expand on ten key features of Pietism to plunge the depths of spiritual renewal for today. The early Pietists were devout German Lutherans. They ignited a Bible-centered movement committed to a heart religion that produces the fruits of faith from a genuine, regenerate life.

They reacted to a sterile and corrupt State Church and demanded pure doctrine matched with a pure life. In the 17th and 18th centuries, Pietism swelled into a torrent of spiritual renewal that influenced the Moravians, the Methodists, the Great Awakenings, the holiness and Pentecostal movements and global evangelicalism.

As lawyers practice law and doctors practice medicine, Pietists practice *piety*. A related term is *pious*. A pious or devout person practices piety. In today's terms, we might say godliness, spirituality or those inner and outer conditions and actions that comprise a life of devotion to God. Piety has a warm and affective side. It exudes humility and virtue, not a stern or stiff side with pursed lips and a creased forehead. I picture piety as on my knees with a downward face and arms wide open, robed in white, drenched in a floodlight of God's favor. Paul advises, "Pursue righteousness, godliness, faith, love, steadfastness, gentleness" (1 Timothy 6:11). The Greek word for *godliness* is *eusebeia*. It refers to respect for deity, translated as "godliness or piety."[16]

I envy fit, elite, Olympic gymnasts, tennis pros and baseball sluggers. They achieved that level by sweat-faced training. I hear Paul use training imagery and bellow, "Roger, train yourself for godliness [piety]; for while bodily training is of some value, godliness [piety] is of value in every way, as it holds promise for the present life and also for the life to come" (1 Timothy 4:7–8). The Greek word for *train* is *gymnazō*, where we get the word *gymnasium*. Paul counsels, "Gymnasium yourself for godliness." He does not say try to be godly but rather train for godliness. As spiritual athletes, let's pursue and train ourselves for piety with the practice of repentance.

The Practice of Repentance

Pietist Philipp Jakob Spener wrote, "The sum of Christianity is repentance, faith, and a new obedience."[17] A spiritual habit in Pietism is *repentance*. Martin Luther taught that the entire life of believers consisted of repentance. Oddly, I do not see this discussed much in books on spiritual formation or in theological training. Jesus summons both unbelievers and believers: "The time is fulfilled, and the kingdom of God is at hand; repent and believe in the gospel" (Mark 1:15). The verbs are present tense—keep on repenting and believing in the Gospel.

Repentance can sound like an austere ordeal imposed on us by a finger-wagging preacher who demands we turn or burn. But repentance is a change of mind with a change of direction. It is a spiritual U-turn with mid-course travel adjustments to face the Lord and stay in the light. If you understand the experience of driving down a dark street, realizing you are lost and need to turn around, you understand repentance. Richard Owen Roberts says, "Repentance is like clearing a highway of holiness to and from God"[18] (see Isaiah 35:8; Luke 3:4–6).

Should not repentance become a spiritual discipline equal in importance and foundational to prayer and solitude, Bible reading and worship?

Peter summons, "Repent therefore, and turn back, that your sins may be blotted out, that times of refreshing may come from the presence of the Lord" (Acts 3:19–20). Today, as I sit at a table on my deck, I face our groomed backyard. The temperature is hot but civil. A cool breeze blows and feels so refreshing, as on a sun-scorched Hawaiian beach. The Greek suggests seasons of cool and refreshing breezes that blow directly from the presence (face) of the Lord. Repentance is the rushing river that moves the hydroelectric turbines of sanctification and renewal.

Repentance is the first word of the Gospel (see Mark 1:15; Acts 2:38) for cleansing from sin (see Psalm 51:2). Like flushing dirty pipes, repentance flushes our hearts of specific sins and impure intentions and preserves the Spirit's presence in our lives (see Psalm 51:11). In corporate settings, we might offer this confession from the *Book of Common Prayer*:

> Most merciful God, we confess that we have sinned against you in thought, word, and deed, by what we have done, and by what we have left undone. We have not loved you with our whole heart; we have not loved our neighbors as ourselves. We are truly sorry and we humbly repent. For the sake of your Son Jesus Christ, have mercy on us and forgive us; that we may delight in your will, and walk in your ways, to the glory of your Name. Amen.[19]

I have a confession. An ingrained sin sometimes reasserts itself in my life. I can nurse corrupt theology. For some nagging reason, I can doubt God is good, that He answers my deepest prayers and that He does consistently what the Bible says He does. Sound like heresy? It is! I routinely repent of these personal heresies when my finite views and circumstances overshadow the holy God.

My corrupt theology can match that of a dedicated Christian couple we know who lost their depressed young daughter to suicide. This tragic event led them to wonder how God could be good. That is a natural response. The lament psalms permit us to wrangle with God. But He is endlessly good and answers prayer. He does what He says, even though our circumstances might scream otherwise. "The LORD is good, a refuge in times of trouble. He cares for those who trust in him" (Nahum 1:7 NIV).

Entrance Liturgy

Years ago, as a green Bible college student, I served as an interim pastor at century-old Olivet Baptist Church in New Westminster, BC. The sanctuary housed a wooden pulpit and pews. A pipe organ bellowed as we sang the lines of this hymn every Sunday service and then prayed:

> Holy, holy, holy! Lord God Almighty!
> Early in the morning our song shall rise to thee.
> Holy, holy, holy, merciful and mighty!
> God in three persons, blessed Trinity.[20]

It reflected the idea of pilgrims in a procession who ready themselves to enter God's holy presence in worship—in piety—with an entrance liturgy.

Enter Psalm 24. It functions as an entrance liturgy that prescribes the rituals or conditions for worshipers in a procession to enter the temple area in Jerusalem—the Lord's mountain and holy place—the sacred site of His manifest presence.

> Who may ascend the mountain of the LORD? Who may stand in his holy place? The one who has clean hands and a pure heart, who does not trust in an idol or swear by a false god. They will receive blessing from the LORD and vindication from God their

Savior. Such is the generation of those who seek him, who seek your face, God of Jacob. Lift up your heads, you gates; be lifted up, you ancient doors, that the King of glory may come in.

Psalm 24:3–7 NIV

Two questions invoke an entrance liturgy of holiness for a presence-centered life. Who may approach and who may continue in God's presence? Those with clean hands and pure hearts whose external conduct and internal character gleam with integrity aloof from idolatry. I am desperate to pursue a presence-centered life in which I seek God's face. This life is one in which the gates that enclose the temple of my heart open wide so the King of *kāvôd* may come in.

4

The Discipline of Awareness

Practicing God's Presence

> We may ignore, but we can nowhere evade, the presence of God. The world is crowded with God. God walks everywhere incognito. And the incognito is not always hard to penetrate. The real labor is to remember, to attend. In fact, to come awake. Still more, to remain awake.
>
> C. S. Lewis[1]

Have you ever used a stone pillow? I have.

One summer Saturday, my wife and I hiked with our daughter and her husband, their four children and their other set of grandparents through the expansive Fish Creek Park in Calgary. Its beauty and terrain provided much-needed exercise and renewal for my sun-baked and breeze-cooled body and soul. With backpacks crammed with snacks and sandwiches, we walked and talked and tossed rocks into the creek. We lunched and laughed, rested and rejoiced, until I was like a yawning old dog who needed a midafternoon snooze.

One problem. Alongside prairie bushes and trees, we parked our picnic on stone-covered ground. Undeterred, I selected a spot to slumber and chose a suitable stone on which to lay my sleepy head. I sawed logs for twenty minutes and awoke to a family ready to go. My wife snapped a photo to document my power nap ingenuity. I reminded her my resourcefulness was biblical and opened God's presence to me. I suppose I am an outdoors type who feels closer to God in nature, in the open-air wild. I named that spot "Bethel by the Creek."

I stole the idea from Jacob (see Genesis 28). Jacob outsmarted his brother, Esau, to get their dad's blessing. Esau plotted to kill him, so Jacob raced for his life. His dad, Isaac, commissioned him to get a wife from Laban and prayed God Almighty would bless him. En route to Haran, Jacob "came to a certain place and stayed there that night, because the sun had set. Taking one of the stones of the place, he put it under his head and lay down in that place to sleep" (verse 11).

Jacob had a vivid dream in which he saw a colossal earth-to-heaven ladder or staircase with angels traveling up and down it. The Lord said to him he was Jacob's God just as he was Abraham's God. He would bless, be with and not leave him (see Genesis 28:10–15). Here is the story's climax:

> When Jacob awoke from his sleep, he thought, "Surely the LORD is in this place, and I was not aware of it." He was afraid and said, "How awesome is this place! This is none other than the house of God; this is the gate of heaven." Early the next morning Jacob took the stone he had placed under his head and set it up as a pillar and poured oil on top of it. He called that place Bethel, though the city used to be called Luz.
>
> Genesis 28:16–19 NIV

Jacob came to "a certain place." A common place. A holy place occupied by the Lord. That site with a stone pillow was a localized gate of heaven—a direct portal into God's presence. Jacob "was not aware of it." When he awoke, fear gripped him. He named that spot Bethel—meaning "house of God." He consecrated it with oil to dedicate it as a divine sanctuary.

Problems of God's Presence

A presence-centered life faces Jacob-style problems. We are all en route to certain places—jobs and errands, appointments and travels, gatherings and respites—unaware God is there. We hold a *formal* theology where we believe God is everywhere. And we hold a *functional* theology where we can live as if He is not, except in church. Ronald Rolheiser writes:

> Rarely is there a sense of God within the bread and butter of life. We still make space for God in our churches, but He is given a very restricted place everywhere else. . . . He is more of a moral and intellectual principle than a person. . . . The struggle to experience God is not so much one of God's presence or absence as it one of the presence or absence of God *in our awareness.* . . . God *is* dead in ordinary consciousness.[2]

And a hurried life can be a vicious felon that squeezes God-awareness out of us. Especially if, like narcissists, we are self-focused and preoccupied with our own awareness.

God is largely hidden and seems to walk incognito, where a coincidence is His way to remain anonymous. Could it be God is perplexingly quiet and shy, like monks, and prefers to commune with us in silence and solitude? This requires we do detailed Sherlock Holmes detective work to uncover clues to God's presence. Holmes said, "You see, but you do not observe."[3] We must observe God's presence in unexpected places.

The magnifying glass of Scripture and the flashlight of the Spirit will help us detect divine evidence left behind. Do you recall times where you later mused, "Wow, God was there, and I wasn't aware of it?" Are we more aware of God's absence than His presence? Like Jesus, let's bypass the crowds and frequently "withdraw to desolate places and pray" (Luke 5:16).

Ramallah and Bethel are near each other geographically. Ramallah, the capital of the Palestinian State, is six miles north of Jerusalem. Bethel is three miles northwest of Ramallah. God commanded Jacob to return there after a series of mishaps. Jacob said to his family:

> "Put away the foreign gods that are among you and purify yourselves and change your garments. Then let us arise and go up to Bethel, so that I may make there an altar to the God who answers me in the day of my distress and has been with me wherever I have gone."
>
> Genesis 35:2–3

Note, "the God who answers me . . . has been with me." These are elements of a Bethel—a house of prayer and presence. The location became a key religious sanctuary in the Old Testament. Throughout history and in modern times, there are actual places that became a Bethel where individuals or groups met God. By the way, our stairway to heaven is not with Led Zeppelin but with Jesus Christ, where we "see heaven opened, and the angels of God ascending and descending on the Son of Man" (John 1:51). He is grander than Jacob (see John 4:12).

Manifestations of God's Presence

Some people have theological problems with specific phrases or practices associated with God's presence. Does God "change the atmosphere" with His presence? Should we "welcome" the Holy Spirit or ask for "more of His presence?" Can an auditorium be "thick" with God, or does God "show up"? Should we pray "God would rend the heavens and come down" so His "glory would fall" in revival?

I value theological hospitality where we welcome diversity in Christian beliefs and expressions if Scripture and the Spirit prevail—Christ-focused, presence-centered. There is room for Anglican and Alliance, Baptist and Brethren, conservative and charismatic, Methodist and Mennonite, Presbyterian and Pentecostal. Like Paul on the Damascus Road and Peter's vision about Cornelius, life-altering encounters with God can shape our theology.

Some of this is theology. Some is terminology or style. The New Covenant ushers in the Spirit's permanent presence who inhabits believers as God's living temples. His indwelling presence works from the inside out with purity and power for sanctification, spiritual gifts and service. He abides *in* us (see John 14:16) and is *with* us (see Matthew 18:20). I recently caught myself praying in a Zoom meeting that Jesus' presence would be *with* us. I corrected myself and affirmed He was already present but prayed He would increase our awareness of Him.

The Spirit is not an impersonal force like Star Wars Jedi knights use. He does not physically change the atmosphere the way billowing smoke from a volcano does. But He can alter the state of entire churches or communities. Reports on revivals in New England or Wales prove that. We might call this pervasive tone an "atmosphere" in which churches or communities are charged with God's presence.

When Jesus taught on prayer (see Luke 11:1–13), He concluded with a promise for more of the Spirit. "If you then, who are evil, know how to give good gifts to your children, how much more will the heavenly Father give the Holy Spirit to those who ask him!" The verb *ask* is present tense—the Father will give the Holy Spirit to those who keep on asking for more of Him. Brazen faith in God's person can neutralize any fear of God's presence.

The New Covenant offers last days outpourings of the Spirit, who fills and fires up believers. These fillings began with Pentecost in Acts 2 and continue until Jesus returns. The Spirit also works from the outside in. An example of this was when an external wind filled the house where believers were, and tongues of fire rested *on* them, enabling them to prophesy (see Acts 2:1–21).

Jesus promised the disciples they would receive power when the Spirit came *upon* them to be His witnesses (see Acts 1:8). The Spirit descended *on* Jesus at His baptism (see Luke 3:22). God pours His Spirit out *on* all flesh with dreams, visions and prophecy (see Acts 2:17–21). We can pray for God's glory to fall just as we pray for His Kingdom to come (see Matthew 6:10). At times we can literally see the Spirit *on* people with His manifest presence.

Sometimes the density of God's presence is so robust that people say it is "thick" or God "showed up." This could mean extraordinary physical or emotional manifestations occurred. Paul describes how the Spirit discloses Himself through spiritual gifts by words of wisdom or knowledge, faith, healings, miracles, tongues, discernment of spirits or prophecy (see 1 Corinthians 12:7–10). Prophecy can awaken unbelievers to God's presence (see 1 Corinthians 14:24–25).

Before Pentecost, the Spirit's presence was evident with Simeon, a righteous and devout Jew who visited baby Jesus at the temple.

> Now there was a man in Jerusalem, whose name was Simeon, and this man was righteous and devout, waiting for the consolation of Israel, and the Holy Spirit was *upon* him. And it had been revealed to him by the Holy Spirit that he would not see death before he had seen the Lord's Christ. And he came in the Spirit into the temple, and when the parents brought in the child Jesus . . .
>
> Luke 2:25–27 (emphasis added)

My holy obsession is that I would be righteous and devout with the Spirit upon me—like Simeon.

Multiple tangible manifestations appear in Scripture and revival accounts. The flesh and the devil can reproduce some, but counterfeits indicate there are genuine expressions to match. Intense times during worship, prayer, proclamation and encounters with God can manifest in fear, awe, dread, heaviness, groans, heightened awareness, stillness, weeping, euphoria, laughter, falling, trembling, shaking, fluttering eyelids, heat, tingling, jolts, an inner glow and an awareness of the numinous. I have experienced many of these, and I am not given to excess or hysteria. For explanations, read my book *Let the River Flow* and John White's book *When the Spirit Comes with Power*.

Examples of manifestations abound in the Old Testament with Moses, Joshua, Gideon, Samuel, Saul, David, Solomon, Elijah, Ezekiel, Daniel and Zechariah. They also abound in the New Testament with Simeon and the disciples and in accounts such as when the place shook where Peter and John and their friends prayed, and the Holy Spirit filled them (see Acts 4:31). Paul received visions and visitations of the Lord in the book of Acts. He also was caught up to the third heaven and could not speak about it (see 2 Corinthians 12:1–7). John "in the Spirit" had a fiery vision of Christ so dramatic he collapsed to his feet as though dead (see Revelation 1:10–17).

Our goal is not to seek manifestations or feel God's presence. We can become preoccupied with the effects rather than the cause. When we are full of the Spirit, however, we will feel joy as Jesus and the early Church did (see Luke 10:21; Acts 13:52). And "You make known to me the path of life; in your presence there is fullness of joy" (Psalm 16:11). The Hebrew is literally "fullness of joy with your face." It refers to a glad satiety like an extravagant and scrumptious festival banquet.[4]

God hard-wired the right side of our brain—the emotional, relational and imaginative side—to govern joy (and love). The

73

left side of our brain is the logical, rational and strategic side—to govern words (and beliefs). Whole-brain Christian life occurs when the left and right sides think in harmony with godly ideas and emotions. When we pursue God's presence—the path of life—this creates the optimum spiritual soil for daily renewal, joy and character formation.[5]

I seek God's presence, not phenomena or impersonal power. We can have subtle brushes with God but not notice them. I aim to become aware of His work inside and outside me through the Spirit's indwelling and manifest presence. Just as contact with an electrical current can cause unusual reactions, it is natural to assume contact with God's manifest presence can cause unusual reactions. But I examine the focus and the fruit.

Reformed Puritan pastor Jonathan Edwards offers five distinguishing marks of a work of the Spirit of God.[6] The Spirit will:

1. Esteem Christ
2. Oppose Satan
3. Regard Scripture
4. Operate as a spirit of truth
5. Operate as a spirit of love to God and people

It is possible to "quench the Spirit" (1 Thessalonians 5:19), grieve the Spirit (Ephesians 4:30), resist the Spirit (Acts 7:51), or outrage the Spirit (Hebrews 10:29). And there are austere times when God's Spirit seems absent.

Absence of God's Presence

On a brilliant sunny Monday afternoon on April 3, 1995, tragedy rocked our world and damaged our souls. My wife and I were babysitting the three little sons of our close friends Tom and Judy. Their oldest boy, Andrew, nearly six, and our sons Joel and Micah played in our front yard. They had invented a contest to see who could run and jump the farthest off the four-foot retaining wall that overlooks a grassy area next to the street.

First Joel jumped, followed by Andrew and Micah. But Andrew fell prostrate and did not get up. Joel ran inside to inform us. Gail retrieved Andrew and carried him into our living room. With his face blue as he lay motionless, we panicked, prayed, called 911 and performed CPR. The paramedics arrived and raced him to the hospital. His mother, Judy, a nurse on duty at Kelowna General Hospital, joined us in the waiting room along with his father, Tom, who had just returned to our place after work.

After a two-hour attempt to revive him and en route to the operating room, the ER doctor returned to inform us Andrew had died. We stood in the lobby stunned and grief-stricken over a freak accident that abruptly ended Andrew's life. It took over two years for us all to rebuild our shattered lives, while Gail and I agonized through an absence of God's presence.

Ponder this quote widely attributed to Simone Weil: "There are only two things that pierce the human heart. One is beauty. The other is affliction."

Pierced, we prayed and pursued God. Theological questions ransacked our minds. *God, where were You? Where are You? Where is Your presence when we need You the most?*

During the dark night of our souls and disappointed with God, our pleas matched some psalmists. "Why have you forsaken me?" (Psalm 22:1). "Why do you hide your face? Why do you forget our affliction and oppression?" (Psalm 44:24). In our naked vulnerability, our entire beings collapsed under the weight of trauma while we sought God. We yelled, "Out of the depths I cry to you, O LORD! O Lord, hear my voice! Let your ears be attentive to the voice of my pleas for mercy! . . . I wait for the LORD, my soul waits, and in his word I hope" (Psalm 130:1–2, 5). We wrestled, "My heart says to you, 'Your face, LORD, do I seek.' Hide not your face from me" (Psalm 27:8–9).

We chose to believe God is still good even when bad things happen to good people, and His love towers above the heavens and outlasts eternity. We chose, as Habakkuk did, to rejoice in Him and reconfirm He is our strength without any tangible reason to do so (see Habakkuk 3:17–19). Like the unseen force of an ocean's undertow, God's unseen force carried us.

All we had was Him. Larry Crabb remarks, "I think it was Tozer who once compared a man complaining that all he had left was God to a fish bemoaning that all it had left was the ocean."[7] A mystery is "Truly, you are a God who hides himself" (Isaiah 45:15). He is here, and we are often not aware. And by the way, we are still good friends with this gracious couple who lost their first-born son on our watch.

While I believe in God's power and the miraculous, a theology of the cross and suffering supersedes a mountain-top triumphalist theology of health and wealth. We live in a Kingdom now-and-not-yet dimension, forced at times to pursue God's presence in lowly heart-wrenching lament. Though we walk through the valley of the shadow of death, God is with us (see Psalm 23:4).

Practices of God's Presence

I heard Bill Johnson preach, "We're designed to recognize presence." But how? James' formula surprises me: "Draw near to God, and he will draw near to you" (James 4:8). Does His nearness depend on me? God still has a conscious relationship with us, though we are unaware of it. "Jesus himself drew near" (Luke 24:15). We might feel as if God is not with us full time, as one seminary student once commented in a case study group I was in.

"The LORD is near to all who call on him, to all who call on him in truth" (Psalm 145:18). How do I draw near to an invisible God who hides? In his book *Reaching for the Invisible God*,

Philip Yancey asks, "How, then, can we have a 'personal rela-tionship' with a God who is invisible, when we're never quite sure he's there?"[8] As a pirate hunts for treasure, let's hunt for God with the practice of God awareness.

Practice God Awareness

On a Monday morning when I was a college student and late for class, I pulled into a packed parking lot at Mount San Antonio College in California. As I sat in my blue Chevy Nova about to open the door, a man wearing a tall jacket and toque walked over and stood there. I opened the window to ask what he wanted. He stuck a long-barrelled pistol in my face. He commanded me not to look at him, to slide over to the pas-senger side and to place my head between my legs. Shock and fear set in!

He drove for ten minutes while I cowered in stunned silence. I prayed two words, "O Lord." Straightway, God's presence settled over me in peace and stillness. My insides relaxed and my heart quit racing. The armed kidnapper stopped, told me to get out and not look back. He had driven to a field near the 57 Freeway onramp. As I stood there, I thought I would get a bullet in my back. But he sped away, and I reeled in confusion as I subconsciously pledged to practice acute God awareness. The police never caught him, but they retrieved my stripped car a week later.

The discipline of awareness assumes God is ever-present. Jesuit Jean-Pierre DeCaussade calls this the "sacrament of the present moment," where self-surrender, stillness and obedience nurture our attention to God's voice and movements in our lives.[9] Gone is the past. Ahead is the future. We live only in the present where God is the perpetual I AM. Gregory Boyd states:

> If God is present in all places at all times, which is what the Bible teaches, then God is part of our surroundings each and

every moment—or as the apostle Paul says, "In him we live and move and have our being" (Acts 17:28). The question is, Are you aware of God surrounding you? Are you awake or asleep to God's presence?[10]

Spiritual guides such as Brother Lawrence, Ronald Rolheiser, Jan Johnson and Rob Reimer help me learn how to practice God's presence, to talk with Him throughout the day and to make my heart a quieted chapel.[11] Jan Johnson offers a relational versus a mechanical approach to meeting with God. Rob Reimer illustrates practicing God's presence as we become more attuned to our spiritual sensitivity. If we walk in the woods, for example, there are birds all around us of which we might not be aware. Odds are we would not be able to detect their different sounds and songs. But if we studied the various kinds of birds in our area with their habits and sounds, we would become more aware of them. We would know what to look and listen for. Nothing changed in the woods, just our attentiveness.[12] We can become more attentive to God's presence as we study His creation. We can apply the Jesuit practice of seeking God in all things. Elizabeth Barrett Browning penned, "Earth's crammed with heaven, and every common bush afire with God."[13]

Richard Lovelace warns, "Deficiency in prayer both *reflects* and *reinforces* inattention to God."[14] The more we neglect prayer, the more we neglect attention to God. And the more we neglect attention to God, the more we neglect prayer. A vicious circle. "And without faith it is impossible to please God, because anyone who comes to him must believe that he exists and that he rewards those who earnestly seek him" (Hebrews 11:6 NIV).

Prayer is a theological issue. Do we behave as if God exists and rewards earnest seekers? God is an extravagant paymaster unlike a paltry Starbucks Rewards Card. He offers the eternal rewards of Himself to those who diligently pursue Him. But we must pay attention to Him. Barbara Brown Taylor remarks:

The practice of paying attention really does take time. Most of us move so quickly our surroundings become no more than blurred scenery we fly past on our way to somewhere else. We pay attention to the speedometer, the wristwatch, the cell phone, the list of things to do, all of which feed our illusion that life is manageable.[15]

One way to increase God awareness is to "pray without ceasing" (1 Thessalonians 5:17), in constant contact with God without intermission. Unceasing prayer is like breathing. "Praying with eyes wide open," remarks Ann Voskamp, "is the only way to pray without ceasing."[16] As I drive, wait in line, load the dishwasher, type on my computer, shovel snow, walk, hold a Zoom meeting and engage in the daily rounds of life, I glance at God and connect with Him. Similar to a well-trained Labrador who glances at its master to get its cues while on walks.

The monastic practice of *statio* is a virtue of presence. It is a practice of transition when we stop one item before we start another, from one activity or meeting to the next. I schedule at least a ten-minute pause to breathe and connect with God between phone calls, Zoom meetings, appointments or other activities.

I pray, "Lord, may your Spirit fill me today and may I host Your presence." As I prepare to read Scripture and pray each morning, I place myself in God's presence. I am learning to talk with God about all things rather than talk to myself with an endless barrage of thoughts. In breath prayer, I inhale a God focus and exhale all else. He might place a thought in my mind, an impression in my heart or an inspiration in my soul. He might send a Scripture verse, an idea or an insight.

Decades ago, while a Ph.D. student at McGill University in Montreal, I received a call from the president of Okanagan Bible College in Kelowna, BC. He invited me to interview for a position I had applied for two years earlier. I learned later the dean graduated from the same seminary as I did and kept my resume on file. After I landed at the Kelowna airport on a February Friday afternoon, I halted on the tarmac and gazed at the snow-speckled hills to the east. I paused and had a sacred awareness, "God is in this place." After the interviews, three words strolled into my mind: "This is it." Six months later, I started as dean of students and instructor.

Little did I know Kelowna would become our personal Bethel, our gate of heaven. Sixteen months later, as a realtor showed me a house, I stood in the living room and looked out the front window at a view overlooking this gleaming city reposed by Okanagan Lake. I paused and recognized His unmistakable presence and those three identical words again: "This is it." We lived there for 22 life-giving years. For the next several decades, God would open direct gateways to His presence in Kelowna and beyond.

Years ago, after a renewal conference at our church, a supremely accurate prophetic person from the team singled me out and announced on Sunday morning, "Roger, God is rearranging your dome." He also reported that he saw me running around the bases at a baseball game with arms spread wide in jubilation. Then he asked with a grin, "Does that mean anything to you?" Stunned, I replied that as a young boy I had hit a home run during a baseball game and rounded the bases with arms spread wide, full of joy!

God seized my attention with this prophetic revelation. And from that day on, He began to enlarge my theology. Like Alice in Wonderland, I fell into God's enchanted Kingdom, vibrant with the Spirit's supernatural presence and gifts, broadcast in 4K resolution and reality.

I worked with worship pastor David Ruis in those years, whose song "Let Your Glory Fall" we belted out. As I ventured into pastoral ministry, I committed myself to spiritual leadership, teaching, writing, church renewal, devotion to prayer and the pursuit of a presence-centered life. God's glory fell regularly.

Practice Enchantment

Cultivate the discipline of awareness where you daily notice and marvel at God's glory in creation—the practice of enchantment. Beauty attracts us. It is crammed into God's glory. "The heavens declare the glory [*kāvôd*] of God, and the sky above proclaims his handiwork" (Psalm 19:1). It is easy to stampede through God's cathedral of creation and become so familiar with it we fail to stay enchanted with its meticulous design and live as if He does not exist.

How can naturalists David Suzuki and Richard Dawkins who celebrate creation remain atheists? The boundless architect fashioned creation, the visible and invisible, from His creative wisdom. Every galaxy and atom, electromagnetic wave, angel, animal, plant and human first existed in God's mind. Mary Oliver writes, "Attention is the beginning of devotion."[17]

One sun-splendored afternoon, my wife, Gail, and I went for a bike ride on nearby walkways. We took a break and sat on a bench as we chatted and observed people walking their dogs. One chap meandered by with a hefty gray-haired Alaskan husky. A few minutes later, a lady trotted by with a pair of miniature brown-haired huskies. I asked the lady about their breed, and she said hers were Australian. I marveled how God was not content to fashion only one breed of husky. There are 22! I Googled and found there are nearly 350 different breeds of dogs!

One winter, as I drove west on my way to Lake Louise to ski with my son-in-law Ryan, I was struck by the snow-crowned Rocky Mountains in the distance. I recalled Psalm 125:2: "As the mountains surround Jerusalem, so the LORD surrounds his people, from this time forth and forevermore." As I went for brisk walks in our snow-blanketed neighborhood, I remembered Isaiah 1:18: "Come now, let us reason together, says the LORD: though your sins are like scarlet, they shall be as white as

81

snow." As I gazed out my home office window during my early morning devotional times, the golden glow of dawn reminded me of Proverbs 4:18: "The path of the righteous is like the light of dawn, which shines brighter and brighter until full day." Adam McHugh reflects, "God spoke creation into existence, and now creation speaks of his existence."[18]

As I walk, I slow down, look around and wonder at God's artistry. Like a Cirque du Soleil extravaganza, opportunities for enchantment abound. Immaculate blue skies, intricate maple leaves, delicate ladybugs and rugged oak trees invite wonder. The dexterity of a human hand and the poise of a grandma's countenance invite awe. Geese in flight and ducks on ponds bid accolades. The Northern Lights summon crescendos of praise. The limitless mastermind who spoke constellations into space left profuse and enthralling clues behind that beckon us to bow before greatness Brené Brown comments on how natural awe and wonder fuel human flourishing:

> Awe and wonder are essential to the human experience. Wonder fuels our passion for exploration and learning, for curiosity and adventure. Researchers have found that awe "leads people to cooperate, share resources, and sacrifice for others" and causes them "to fully appreciate the value of others and see themselves more accurately, evoking humility." Some researchers even believe that "awe-inducing events may be one of the fastest and most powerful methods of personal change and growth."[19]

Years ago, as a young pastor during a church retreat at Green Bay Bible Camp in West Kelowna, I first practiced enchantment. Alone, I ambled down to the dock on Okanagan Lake. I lay flat on my back to gaze into the star-crowded midnight sky. Ten minutes in, I asked God to shoot a star across the sky. Two minutes later, one streamed from right to left. I paused and braved another request. I asked God, if this was actually

Him, would He shoot another star from left to right—the opposite direction? Two minutes later, one streamed from left to right. I was astounded with God's X-ray penetration as His presence exhilarated my quivering soul. A coincidence or a God incognito? A rampant imagination or a Bethel encounter? The discipline of awareness.

PART 2

EXPERIENCING GOD'S PRESENCE

5

Spirit-Saturation and Fire

Presence-Centered Power and Purity

> What is it that inevitably happens when one is baptized by the Lord Jesus Christ with the Holy Spirit? A sense of the glory of God, an unusual sense of the presence of God.
>
> Martin Lloyd-Jones[1]

Celia was a saint who pursued God's presence.

When I traveled to Edmonton for some of my district minister work, I would stay at the home of Celia and Gerald, an elderly Christian couple. Celia, a Ukrainian, and Gerald, a Newfoundlander, dazzled everyone with their rare combination of stubborn wit and wisdom as they served their Baptist church and their neighbors with equal impact. Celia's forte was women's Bible studies and hospitality. She offered steady supplies of homemade bread, buns, cookies and muffins. And borscht. She also offered prayer. The aroma of baked goods that wafted through her home matched the aroma of her prayers that wafted through heaven. Though Celia had fought off cancer, it returned with a vengeance a second time.

One cheery Saturday afternoon, I visited them. As we chatted over English tea and oatmeal cookies, I wanted to pray God would heal Celia. Instead, I thought I should ask how I could pray for her. She glanced my way with a beaming smile and blurted, "Pray I would be filled with the Holy Spirit!" Stunned, I chuckled. After I regathered myself, I prayed for that and witnessed God's Spirit endow her with tranquility and joy. She died three months later at age 86. I was honored to officiate at her funeral and give the message. I suppose she died full of God's Spirit and presence. With dementia, sadly, Gerald died three years later at age 92.

The Holy Spirit and God's Presence

When I near the finish line, what prayer will I cherish? Is the Spirit's fullness bursting in me? Some Ephesian-type believers might not even know there is a Holy Spirit (see Acts 19:2). Others might avoid, neglect, minimize or consign Him to charismatics or Pentecostals.

Pentecostals are six hundred million strong worldwide. Must we become Pentecostals or charismatics to experience the Spirit's fullness? Is not God wider? I often meet self-labeled "bapticostals" or "closet charismatics" who encounter the Spirit undercover. Scores of Christians journey in and out of conservative and charismatic contexts where extremes or errors burn or confuse them. While experiences attributed to the Spirit can draw criticism, are they not usually aimed at the extremes and errors or at weirdness and wildness? Should we define the center by the fringe? Countless disappointments abound. Bradley Jersak offers perspective:

> Whether it's the "fire" of Evangelical revivalism, the Pentecostal two-step, tongues-speaking "charismania," the "prayer lines" of the renewal movement, or the politicized "prophets," who are still ranting away, I can testify firsthand that the sought-after "Presence" is not always so sweet. . . . In my case, a lateral move from charismatic to contemplative practice helped me retain my life in the Spirit, draining away the adrenaline hangovers and easing off the compulsion to "press in." I could rest in the Spirit who has *already* been *poured out on all flesh . . . and everywhere present, rather than hoping . . . that I could "pull down heaven"* like the frantic prophets of Baal. I can even worship as a small-c charismatic again.[2]

And me? I am a Pietist who pursues God's presence with Spirit saturation and fire. May our souls smolder with spiritual audacity and ardor. "Do not be slothful in zeal, be fervent in spirit [or in the Spirit], serve the Lord" (Romans 12:11). There are, however, those who are overly crazed with the Spirit. Some pursue conferences and churches that offer decisive encounters to receive the blessing or anointing with heightened euphoria. Their theology and format tend to come from revivalist or charismatic traditions. While others are overly cautious with the Spirit and tend to avoid such encounters. Their theology and format tend to come from reformed or conservative traditions.

Scripture showcases both—ecstatic encounters and unsensational plodding. But the overall conversion process is slow, incremental and gradual. It takes time for the Spirit, Scripture and Sacraments to form us into Jesus' likeness. As we tend gardens, we must tend our souls deeply to live by the Spirit.[3]

Why is our culture fascinated with the paranormal and experiential, especially Millennials (those born in 1980–2000)? Why did the books *Conversations with God* and *Harry Potter* generate such interest? And the movie series *Twilight* and the television series *Game of Thrones*?

What drew crowds to Jesus? Was it not His proclamation of the Kingdom confirmed through healing and deliverance (see Matthew 4:23–25)? Diana Butler Bass observes, "In the Global South, they struggle to keep up with the Spirit; in the West, we struggle to embrace it."[4]

Behaving and Believing in the Holy Spirit

With the Apostles Creed—the oldest Church confession—we can announce, "I believe in the Holy Spirit." May my life blare more than this. May I *behave* in the Holy Spirit! The Spirit floodlights Jesus. As the truth giver and guider, His purpose is to glorify Him (see John 16:13–14).

The Spirit holds a central and visible role in the Trinity's life and mission, not secondary or anonymous. The word *Spirit*, when connected to the Holy Spirit, appears nearly 250 times in the New Testament and 57 times in the book of Acts. The Hebrew term *rûah* and the Greek term *pneuma* mean *wind* or *breath*—wind in motion. In reference to God's Spirit, they mean His power, energy and life in motion. As co-equal and co-eternal, the Holy Spirit as God is not a junior member of the Trinity. R. T. Kendall remarks, "The presence of the Lord and the Holy Spirit are the same thing. And yet we have seen that people do not always sense His presence even when He is present."[5]

I taught a seminary course on the presence-centered life. Later, a student relayed to me that the manifest presence of God had been immensely powerful during a specific experience. She relayed how, as she met with friends over Zoom, they spent some time in worship and intentionally invited the Lord's presence. They felt led into an extended time of prayer, and the Lord's manifest presence descended on all of them. She shared it felt like heavy air filled with moisture. They received a vision of a waterfall comprised of both fire and water. She put her hand in the waterfall and experienced both burning and refreshing. Her reaction to the experience was to fully step into the waterfall.

The 2/3 God

Released in 2009, Francis Chan's book *The Forgotten God: Reversing Our Tragic Neglect of the Holy Spirit* was a bestseller. Why? Since then, a steady stream of books on the Holy Spirit have appeared. Why? Are we Trinitarians who worship the Father, follow the Son and live by the Spirit? Or are we binitarians who are unaware of the Spirit? Must we recover one-third of the Godhead in our faith and life? Do we believe in the Father, Son and Holy Scriptures and worship a 2/3 God? How vibrant is the Spirit's presence in your life and church? "The presence of the Spirit, as an experienced and living reality," states Gordon Fee, "was the crucial matter for Christian life, from beginning to end."[6] A report of the Cultural Research Center at Arizona Christian University discovered that, of the self-identified born-again Christians polled, "58% contend that the Holy Spirit is not a real, living being but is merely a symbol of God's power, presence, or purity."[7] The Spirit is a sensitive Person, not a vague power.

Well documented is the decline of church vitality and attendance in the United States and Canada over the last several decades. A growing segment is the "nones and dones" who have no religion or are done with it. Discouraged pastors might resort to more church growth and leadership training to invigorate hollow church life. Churches that become greenhouses steaming with the Spirit's presence in fullness and fire will unleash luxuriant growth and vitality. Do we sit with a vertical, rational faith, cloistered in sterile ideas like a white-gowned scientist tamed of mystery and miracle? Or do we run with a horizontal, dynamic faith like an untamed cheetah in the holy wild, explosive and free? Our culture yearns for the supernatural—not the cerebral—with an untamed God.

Modernist Western culture and Christians tend to distrust the supernatural. But is it satisfying to simply think about God? Do we not crave direct encounters with Him? In his outstanding book *When Everything's on Fire*, Brian Zahnd critiques abstract, cerebral Christianity and offers a blueprint on how to build a theological house of the heart by a revelation of Christ and His love through the Spirit (see Ephesians 3:14–19). He suggests we read the gospels on our knees for six months. And before each chapter, ask Jesus to reveal Himself to us. And decide what to do with Him and act on it, not simply think about it. Jesus self-authenticates His teaching when we resolve to do God's will (see John 7:17).[8] Try it. I did. Risky, but rewarding.

Spirit-Saturated Jesus

The Holy Spirit age erupted at Jesus' baptism. Imagine the scene: John—the burly Elijah-style prophet—baptized throngs of sinners with the chilly Jordan River waters in the scorching Judean desert. Jesus approached His cousin. All four gospels record this incident. But Luke, who shows a special interest in the Spirit's role and prayer with Jesus and with the early Church, reports:

> Now when all the people were baptized, and when Jesus also had been baptized and was praying, the heavens were opened, and the Holy Spirit descended on him in bodily form, like a dove; and a voice came from heaven, "You are my beloved Son; with you I am well pleased."
>
> Luke 3:21–22

The Trinity cooperates together where Jesus is ordained as the royal Son of God for Messianic ministry with the Spirit's anointing (see Psalm 2:7; Isaiah 61:1).

The Open Heaven

After John baptized Jesus, while Jesus prayed, the heavens split wide open, and the Holy Spirit descended on Him in a visible, bodily form. Notice the fusion of prayer and presence. Jesus stood there saturated with water and Spirit. The heavens now remain open with direct access. How? Before his martyrdom, Stephen "full of the Holy Spirit, gazed into heaven and saw the glory of God, and Jesus standing at the right hand of God. And he said, 'Behold, I see the *heavens opened*, and the Son of Man standing at the right hand of God'" (Acts 7:55–56, emphasis added). The verb for *opened* is perfect tense, which signifies completed action with permanent results.

Jesus said to Nathanael, "You will see *heaven opened*, and the angels of God ascending and descending on the Son of Man" (John 1:51, emphasis added). Luke reports, "Peter went up on the housetop about the sixth hour to pray. And he became hungry and wanted something to eat, but while they were preparing it, he fell into a trance and saw the *heavens opened* and something like a great sheet descending, being let down by its four corners upon the earth" (Acts 10:9–11, emphasis added). Both texts are in the perfect tense. As McDonald's restaurants remain open 24/7, the heavens remain open 24/7. Bill Johnson declares, "Every believer has an open Heaven. For the believer, most closed heavens are between the ears. . . . We always reflect the nature of the world we are most aware of. Living aware of open heavens has incalculable results."[9]

As I drove from Home Depot one afternoon in my Honda CRV, with Red Rocks's live worship "My Deliverer" blaring through the sound system, the gleaming blue sky caught my eyes. I clenched the steering wheel and hollered to God, "There's an open heaven up there! God, by Your Spirit, we have unlimited access to one another anytime, anywhere!" I prayed for the Spirit to saturate me. His presence swirled in my car.

The Spirit and Jesus

Jesus began His ministry as a thirty-year-old young adult (see Luke 3:23). The Spirit saturated and stayed with Him (see verse 22), filled Him and led Him into His desert test (see 4:1), and empowered and anointed Him (see 4:14, 18). Jesus, fully God and fully human, did not pull rank and muster His divine power to gain an edge over sin, sickness, Satan and nature. He relied on the Spirit's power and God's favor with Him. Luke documents:

> "You yourselves know what happened throughout all Judea, beginning from Galilee after the baptism that John proclaimed: how God anointed Jesus of Nazareth with the Holy Spirit and with power. He went about doing good and healing all who were oppressed by the devil, for God was with him."
>
> Acts 10:37–38

Note the link between presence and power. As a limited, though sinless, entirely human young adult, Jesus had to rely on the Spirit whom God gave without measure (see John 3:34). The passages in Luke and Acts establish patterns that drive a presence-centered life for us. Scot McKnight concludes:

> Jesus was the Spirit-filled human among humans. . . . To be a follower of Jesus is to be open to the same Spirit to whom Jesus was wide open. The good news is that the Spirit at work in Jesus is available to us. Are you open to the Spirit as Jesus was open?[10]

I am open.

Spirit-Saturated Saints

Before Jesus' baptism, John answered a crowd buzzing with questions about whether he might be Christ. He yells:

> I baptize you with water, but he who is mightier than I is coming, the strap of whose sandals I am not worthy to untie. He will

baptize you with the Holy Spirit and fire. His winnowing fork is in his hand, to clear his threshing floor and to gather the wheat into his barn, but the chaff he will burn with unquenchable fire.

Luke 3:16–17

Holy Purity

To *baptize* is to plunge or wash for ceremonial purification or dip for dedication and initiation. It means to immerse. In classical Greek, it can refer to sunken ships. Jesus saturates us with the Spirit and fire to dedicate and purify us. I have watched expectant believers clamor for the baptism of the Holy Spirit, but what about the baptism of fire?

Jesus' baptism with the Holy Spirit and fire supersedes John the Baptist's baptism with water. Farmers used a winnowing fork-like shovel to throw the wheat and chaff (straw) into the air so the wind would separate the lighter chaff from the heavier wheat as it fell to the threshing floor. They would use the chaff as fuel to burn in an oven. Notice, the baptism of fire is *unquenchable*. It continues to burn and eliminate worthless chaff from our lives and purify us in holiness. Holy fire purges and refines us (see Zechariah 13:9; 1 Peter 1:7). At Pentecost, Jesus baptized the 120 disciples with the Spirit, accompanied by the sound of a mighty rushing wind and divided tongues or lapping flames of fire upon each one (see Acts 2:1–4).

Holy Power

Fast forward to Luke 24. After His resurrection, Jesus appeared to startled disciples in Jerusalem. And over a broiled fish dinner, He offered a Scripture lesson with a Gospel commission (see verses 36–48). As they swallowed and listened, Jesus concluded, "I am sending the promise of my Father upon you. But stay in the city until you are clothed with power from on high" (verse 49). This reminds me of Gideon, who faced the dire threat of Midianite and Amalekite armies and "the Spirit of the LORD clothed Gideon" (Judges 6:34). With a downsized army of three hundred, he quashed them. I love being clothed with new shirts from Costco. But imagine God clothing you with Himself with His power from on high. Bound to surpass Costco in impact!

Over to the book of Acts. Luke forecasts Pentecost:

> And while staying with them [Jesus] ordered them not to depart from Jerusalem, but to wait for the promise of the Father, which, he said, "you heard from me; for John baptized with water, but you will be baptized with the Holy Spirit not many days from now."
>
> Acts 1:4–5

And "You will receive power when the Holy Spirit has come upon you, and you will be my witnesses in Jerusalem and in all Judea and Samaria, and to the end of the earth" (verse 8). Spirit-powered witness includes signs and wonders.

Many churches do not see God's manifest power that erupts from daring prayer and proclamation. It is easier to play it safe with controlled doctrine and avoid risk or controversy. But that is not what we see in the gospels and Acts. The early Church prayed for supernatural power to join their speaking.

> "And now, Lord, look upon their threats and grant to your servants to continue to speak your word with all boldness, while you stretch out your hand to heal, and signs and wonders are performed through the name of your holy servant Jesus."
>
> Acts 4:29–30

I dare you to pray such audacious prayers!

Holy Prayer

The disciples started a ten-day rooftop prayer meeting in a Jerusalem home. A motley band of fishermen, family and friends, which swelled to 120, gathered. "All these with one accord were devoting themselves to prayer, together with the women and Mary the mother of Jesus, and his brothers" (Acts 1:14). The last mention of mother Mary and the women is at this prayer meeting! Is it not often faithful mothers and women who attend prayer meetings? The Greek word for *one accord* is *homothumadon*. It means "with one mind, unanimously, and one passion."[11] United prayer acts like a battering ram with God's promises until breakthrough. Armin Gesswein, who prayed for and served with Billy Graham, said, "When Jesus went back to heaven, all He left behind was a prayer meeting."[12]

Holy Pentecost

What John prophesied in Luke 3 and Jesus reiterated in Acts 1 hurricaned down from the open heaven in tangible manifestations of God's presence.

> When the day of Pentecost arrived, they were all together in one place. And suddenly there came from heaven a sound like a mighty rushing wind, and it filled the entire house where they were sitting. And divided tongues as of fire appeared to them and rested on each one of them. And they were all filled with the Holy Spirit and began to speak in other tongues as the Spirit gave them utterance.
>
> Acts 2:1–4

Luke substitutes the word *filled* for *baptized* and *clothed*, making them synonymous. From Pentecost on, we see the repeatable New Covenant age of the Spirit pattern first modeled by Jesus. He deploys the Spirit and baptizes/clothes/fills receptive believers with His manifest presence and power. According to Acts 1:8 combined with Peter's sermon in Acts 2:17–21, the evidence of this filling is prophetic witness to Christ. As the fulfillment of Joel 2:28–32, God pours out His Spirit on boys and girls, teens, adults and elderly who shall prophesy with revelatory speech in these last days (see Acts 2:17–18). Tongues can accompany the deluge. They were known human languages those believers had not learned. Different than Acts 2, Paul discusses a variety of unknown heavenly prayer and prophetic tongues in 1 Corinthians 12–14.

Peter thunders a message about Jesus the ascended baptizer, "Being, therefore exalted at the right hand of God, and having received from the Father the promise of the Holy Spirit, he has poured out this that you yourselves are seeing and hearing" (Acts 2:33). With Luke, Jesus baptizes/clothes/fills believers with the Spirit for power in prophetic witness. With Paul, the Spirit baptizes all believers at regeneration into the Body of Christ and to drink from the indwelling Spirit. "For we were all baptized by one Spirit so as to form one body—whether Jews or Gentiles, slave or free—and we were all given the one Spirit to drink" (1 Corinthians 12:13 NIV). There is one water baptism into Christ, "One Lord, one faith, one baptism" (Ephesians 4:5; Romans 6:3–4).

Peter states, "The Spirit of glory [*doxa*] and of God rests upon you" (1 Peter 4:14). *Rests* is present tense, where the same Spirit that rested on Jesus (see Matthew 3:16) continues to also rest on us. This echoes Isaiah 11:2, "And the Spirit of the LORD shall rest upon him, the Spirit of wisdom and understanding, the Spirit of counsel and might, the Spirit of the knowledge and fear of the LORD." What is true of Jesus is true of all Christians.

Luke reports smaller-scale examples that occurred after Pentecost when the Holy Spirit *fell on* people. Peter and John prayed for the Samaritans to receive the Holy Spirit, for He had not fallen on them. They laid their hands on them and they received the Holy Spirit (see Acts 8:14–17). Then, Luke continues to report this repeating post-Pentecost pattern in Acts 10:44–47, 11:15–17 and 19:1–7.

I regularly pray for the Spirit to fill and fall on people. It is remarkable to watch. It is temporary and repeatable. I have received prayer with the laying-on-of-hands, and I practice that with others, too, with prayers of impartation like Peter and John did with the Samaritans. Ananias laid hands on Paul, and the Spirit filled him (see Acts 9:17). A council of elders imparted a gift to Timothy with prophecy and laying-on-of-hands (see 1 Timothy 4:14). Moses laid hands on and commissioned Joshua "in whom is the Spirit" (Numbers 27:18).

I urge church leaders to pray for the Spirit to fill new believers during their baptisms. When I was a Vineyard pastor, I prayed for a young man I baptized in Okanagan Lake. As he rose from the water, spurting and shaking, a demon manifested. I cast it out right there in the lake! He waded back to shore filled with the Spirit and free! When I was a Vernon Alliance pastor, we arranged for elders to pray for people, soaking wet from their baptisms, to become soaked with the Spirit. One girl fell backwards in the tub when the Spirit rushed on her!

My initial Spirit saturation occurred several weeks after I gave my life to Christ. I sat alone on my bed in the barracks on a cold, sunny Saturday morning at Fort Lewis, Washington, as a new US soldier and new believer in Christ. I remember reading John's gospel. A torrent of impeccable energy rushed into every room of my soul. The movie *On Golden Pond* captures what it was like for me in the scene where young Billy raced around the magical Squam Lake alone in a Chris Craft motorboat, enthralled, grinning, with outstretched arms. Over the years, I have had multiple Spirit fillings in private and public settings.

Filling and Fullness

The filling of the Spirit is spontaneous and temporary. For *filled* Luke uses the word *pimplēmi*. It is an external, dynamic Spirit saturation that comes *upon* believers matched with power and boldness in proclamation. Picture a hot shower that flows *on* you. The believers were filled with the Spirit and spoke in tongues (see Acts 2:4). Peter, filled with the Spirit, spoke with wisdom to the rulers (see Acts 4:8). When they prayed, the place where they gathered shook, and they were filled with the Spirit and spoke God's word boldly (see Acts 4:31). These fillings are temporary and repeatable. They activate God's manifest presence as needed in the moment. Wrath, fury, jealousy and confusion can fill people (see Luke 4:28; 6:11; Acts 5:17; 19:29). What fills you?

There is also the fullness of the Spirit, which is static and long-term. For *full*, Luke uses the word *plērēs*. He is the only writer who uses the phrase "full of the Spirit." It is an internal, permanent Spirit saturation that resides *in* believers for spirituality, sometimes paired with faith. It describes character and effect, which is *Spirit*-ual, lush with the Fruit of the Spirit (see Galatians 5:22–23). Imagine Spirit rivers that flow *in* you. Picture yourself like Jesus "full of the Holy Spirit, returned from the Jordan" (Luke 4:1), and Barnabas "a good man, full of the Holy Spirit and of faith" (Acts 11:24), and Stephen, "a man full of faith and of the Holy Spirit . . . full of grace and power, was doing great wonders and signs among the people," and "gazing at him, all who sat in the council saw that his face was like the face of an angel" (Acts 6:5, 8, 15). I long to be full of the Holy Spirit and faith with an angelic face. I pray for Spirit-saturated character and effect.

Paul uses the verb *plēroō*. "And do not get drunk with wine . . . but be *filled* with the Spirit" (Ephesians 5:18, emphasis added). This is a present passive verb with a communal focus where we let ourselves be continually filled with the Spirit along with others. He calls believers to let themselves be continually controlled by the Spirit in corporate worship and mutual submission.

Note the connection between filled by the Spirit, singing and gratitude:

> Addressing one another in psalms and hymns and spiritual songs, singing and making melody to the Lord with your heart,

giving thanks always and for everything to God the Father in the name of our Lord Jesus Christ, submitting to one another out of reverence for Christ.

Ephesians 5:19–21

Do you remember that dinner party with Lazarus, Mary, Martha and Jesus, where Mary anointed Jesus' feet with expensive ointment? To anoint a guest with oil was a gesture of hospitality. Its fragrance *filled* the house (see John 12:3). The word *filled* is the same word Paul used in Ephesians 5:18 when he urged us to be filled with the Spirit. I long for churches to be filled with the Spirit's fragrance. Let's use Fred Hartley's prayer for the Spirit's filling and fullness:

I wade in the waters of Your presence. I relinquish control to You. I yield my rights and privileges to You. Take me and fill me. Take control of my mind, will and emotions. Take control. Baptize me. Immerse me. Saturate me. Spirit, soul and body. Take back from the enemy any ground I have given over. Father, right now I receive the fullness of the Holy Spirit in the name of the Lord Jesus Christ. Amen.[13]

Spirit-ual Life and Leadership

I taught a course called Essentials of Pastoral Care at Taylor Seminary. I argued that effective pastoral care and counseling, preaching and prayer depend on the extent to which we lead by the Spirit. I asked students, "What's a spiritual leader?" After vague responses, I offered this: "A spiritual leader is someone who's led, formed and empowered by the Spirit and who leads by the Spirit not the flesh." I jotted on the whiteboard: "When we live and walk by the Spirit and not by the flesh, we are *Spirit*-ual." Un-spiritual people live and lead by natural and carnal means, not by the Spirit (see 1 Corinthians 2:13–15; 3:1; Romans 8:5–14). We lead more by character and presence than by leadership skills, and we must learn to recognize the Spirit. I cited Alan Nelson: "Given the human propensity to live out of our own strengths as opposed to relying on the Spirit, giving in to the dominate emotions of anger, revenge, control, and intimidation are symptomatic of non-spiritual leading."[14]

Live and Walk by the Spirit

One student sheepishly asked, "How do we do this?"

I replied, "Turn to Galatians 5:16." I read, "But I say, walk by the Spirit, and you will not gratify the desires of the flesh." This means to continuously conduct our lives by the Spirit's influence. We reviewed the rotten works of the flesh in verses 19–21 and contrasted the luscious fruit of the Spirit in verses 22–23.

Christian spirituality is *social*. It is faith active through love as the law's fulfillment (see Galatians 5:6, 13–14). As we walk by the Spirit, His fruit benefits others in how they experience us: love, joy, peace, patience, kindness, goodness, faithfulness, gentleness and self-control (see verses 22–23).

We ended on verse 25: "If we live by the Spirit, let us also keep in step with the Spirit." The *source* is live by the Spirit. The *course* is keep in step with the Spirit. As a military term, it means to walk in a straight line and follow a rule, like follow the leader. The present tense suggests a march to the Spirit's cadence in following His directions. We do not activate a Spirit-saturated life by natural means. Human formulas or techniques will run aground.

Posture and Practices

I suggest one posture and two practices. First, surrender, then pray and receive.

Surrender. When we drive and approach an on-ramp, we might see an inverted red triangle Yield sign. It means to wait and let others proceed before we enter that highway. This illustrates a posture of surrender for *Spirit*-ual life. Based on the book of Colossians, I wrote *Magnificent Surrender* to explore this posture in detail. The spiritual life is the surrendered life. Nancy Leigh DeMoss writes, "It is in the laboratory of life that our initial consecration to Christ is tested, proven, and demonstrated in daily, moment-by-moment choices and responses, as we surrender to the sovereignty and will of God."[15] Surrender enables spiritual formation—being formed by the Spirit. Watch Hillsong's live YouTube worship song "I Surrender" with lyrics.

Pray. As He prayed, the Spirit descended on Jesus (see Luke 3:21–22). As they waited, the disciples prayed and were filled (see Acts 1:14). After Jesus taught on prayer, He asked, "How much more will the heavenly Father give the Holy Spirit to those who ask him!" (Luke 11:13). Prayer warrior Armin Gesswein declares, "There's no record in Scripture, or anywhere else, of anyone who was filled with the Spirit who was not a very *prayerful* person . . . or of anyone *continuing* to live as a Spirit-filled person who doesn't *continue* to be a very prayerful person."[16]

Receive. To live by the Spirit's filling and fullness is to actively receive, not resist, the real, living Holy Spirit as a *person* as you would welcome a dignitary. On resurrection day, Jesus met with His disciples. He "breathed on them and said to them, 'Receive the Holy Spirit'" (John 20:22). The Greek word for *receive* is *lambanō.* It means to "lay hold of, to take up."[17] Jesus promises the personal Spirit to those who receive or clutch Him by faith (see Galatians 3:2). I encourage you to memorize these passages that refer to receiving the personal Holy Spirit: John 7:39; Acts 2:38; 8:14–19; 19:2.

On the last day of class, I rallied the students to walk by the Spirit's luminous filling and fullness. I prayed, then waited. One student became overwhelmed. Slumped in his chair with wide eyes, he blurted, "Oh, wow, I feel like I'm on fire!" The other students sat motionless as God's presence settled in. That was a sacred encounter. We left aglow. I regularly pray for Spirit saturation and fire—for fillings, fullness and the Fruit of the Spirit for power and purity.

6

Continual Fire on the Altar

Presence-Centered Prayer

Fire shall be kept burning on the altar continually; it shall not go out.

Leviticus 6:13

What can God do through a 26-year-old Austrian Lutheran?

In 1738 the poet Isaac Watts wrote a letter of recommendation to the president of Harvard College. "He is a Person of uncommon Zeal and Piety, and of an Evangelic Spirit."[1] This person was the Christ-centered, Spirit-saturated, missional Pietist who led the Moravians—Count Nicholas Ludwig von Zinzendorf (1700–1760).

In 1722 he founded a colony of Christian refugees on the east German border. Called *Herrnhut* ("under the Lord's watch"), it flourished as a community of Moravian Pietism. By the fifth year, dissension poisoned its 220 members. On May 12, 1727, Zinzendorf drafted a *Brotherly Agreement* that cured the factions. That ensuing "golden summer of 1727" became a habitation of God where a spirit of prayer seized the community, including children. During prayer, many sunk down, and *Herrnhut* became an inferno of God's presence.

On August 13, 1727, during a communion service, *Herrnhut* experienced a "Moravian Pentecost." The Spirit flowed in signs and wonders and into their hearts with a flaming love. The nearness of Christ was so tangible to all, even two workers twenty miles away and unaware of the meeting became deeply conscious of the same effects. On August 27, they established a 24/7 non-stop prayer watch with 48 men and women who prayed in pairs hourly inspired by one Scripture-fed verse: "Fire shall be kept burning on the altar continually; it shall not go out."[2]

Known as the "hourly intercession," that prayer burned for over a century! Powered by *homothumadon* prayer, the Moravians ignited the first large-scale Protestant global missionary movement primarily of laypeople. By 1791, they catapulted three hundred missionaries worldwide, established over thirty settlements globally on the *Herrnhut* model, and spawned hundreds of small renewal groups that operated within the existing churches of Europe known as *Diaspora Societies*. With Gibraltar faith, Zinzendorf altered the course of Christianity.

This all started in early 1727 when 26-year-old Zinzendorf and others covenanted to pray and labor for revival. His motto: "I have one passion: it is Jesus, Jesus only."[3]

Zinzendorf and the Moravians at *Herrnhut* stoke my passion for presence-centered prayer. Though the image of fire on the altar primarily refers to sacrifice, it complements the image of continual prayer as burning incense before God. David sings, "Let my prayer be counted as incense before you, and the lifting up of my hands as the evening sacrifice" (Psalm 141:2). As the fragrance of backyard BBQs and perfume boutiques waft into our nostrils, the fragrance of continual sacrifice mingled with prayer wafts into God's presence.

In Revelation 5:8, the 24 elders each hold a harp (worship) and golden bowls full of incense, which are the prayers of the saints. Absorb this:

> And another angel came and stood at the altar with a golden censer, and he was given much incense to offer with the prayers of all the saints on the golden altar before the throne, and the smoke of the incense, with the prayers of the saints, rose before God from the hand of the angel. Then the angel took the censer and filled it with fire from the altar and threw it on the earth, and there were peals of thunder, rumblings, flashes of lightning, and an earthquake.
>
> Revelation 8:3–5

Problems of Prayer

In his book *Your God Is Too Safe*, Mark Buchanan suggests prayer can seem like mere smoke and scent, an aromatic vapor. Yet it contains atomic potential. And the discipline of prayer is not primarily about bargaining with or getting things from God but about *waiting*—for God to act—"for the fire to ignite the incense, waiting for perfume to be made into bombs."[4] Picture those inverted cones that collect water at a water park or pool to reach a tipping point as we wait. There is a coming tipping point as we wait on God while He collects our prayers in heaven.

As I read Leviticus and Revelation, I imagine my heart as an altar of fire with an eternal flame. In the inspiring song "Flames," Matt Redman sings of the altar of our heart—with a burning sacrifice within—which would rise as an everlasting flame of worship to God.

I was one of four speakers at a pastors and spouses retreat for ministry resiliency. In the afternoon, we debriefed and prayed as a team in an upstairs room for the final evening session. One leader shared how he saw a prophetic vision of a flame descend from heaven. As soon as he said it, God's presence pierced my soul, and I dropped to my knees in the fear of God. I assumed God would land on everyone in fire power.

In that final session, we prayed and offered prophecies and words of knowledge for each person. Then they prayed for each team member. Tears and sacred astonishment flowed. They prayed for me last. In minutes, my entire body sweltered. The room's temperature was not hot, and yet perspiration seeped through my shirt. I felt several jolts and became limp in sublime wonder and joy. The flame of heaven descended and ignited that room while it incited my passion for prayer in pursuing God's presence.

Richard Foster recounts how his hand grew extremely warm when he placed it on a man's chest while he prayed for his deep healing. And he mentions Richard Rolle's book, *The Fire of Divine Love*, in which he describes unusual experiences of God's intense heat around his heart.[5] God can literally warm our hands, hearts and bodies as a physical manifestation of his healing and empowering presence generated by prayer.

The Challenge of Prayer

But prayer, like diets and exercise, is easy to preach but arduous to practice. It is a challenge to communicate with an invisible God on His terms. He is quiet and often replies in cryptic and elusive ways. Sometimes, the words *prayer* or *prayer meeting* can recruit as much enthusiasm as the word *chore*. For some, prayer is a dull regimen, an unsavory discipline, like having to eat your broccoli as a kid because it was good for you. Or as a private, "devo" time, distracted as "weird associations jump about in [your] mind like monkeys in a banana tree."[6] Be cheered, for "the Spirit helps us in our weakness. For we do not know what to pray for as we ought, but the Spirit himself intercedes for us with groanings too deep for words" (Romans 8:26).

Prayer reminds some people of heaven-sounding excursions of religious words that drone on with checklists of requests for traveling mercies, Aunt Nancy's hip surgery and final exams, prefaced by lots of talk while sitting in a circle with others on wooden chairs under glaring lights. Brian Stiller of the World Evangelical Alliance remarked to me, "For many, prayer is an agenda item rather than a strategic resource to advance God's Kingdom."

David Butts, president of Harvest Prayer Ministries says, "The reason most people do not attend prayer meetings at their church is that they have been to prayer meetings at their church."[7] Lord, have mercy! Revive us!

I should pray because Moses and David prayed, Jesus and the early Church prayed, and "All who have walked with God have viewed prayer as the main business of their lives."[8] I have a prayer life, but do I have a life of prayer? I have experimented with various methods, read over eighty books, and studied the Bible on prayer. Several years ago, I devoted myself to prayer (see Acts 6:4; Colossians 4:2). The Greek word for *devote* is *proskartereite*. It means to "persist obstinately, be busily engaged in."[9]

I dove into the deep end to try unceasing prayer (see 1 Thessalonians 5:17). The Greek word for *unceasing* is *adialeiptōs* and means, "constantly, continually, without intermission."[10]

I aim to practice persistent, ceaseless, presence-centered prayer. For assistance, see the *Daily Prayer* and *Lectio 365* apps. But, as New Year's resolutions lose steam in February, I lose steam to keep the fire burning on the altar continually. D. A. Carson offers lesson one: "We do not drift into disciplined prayer. We will not grow in prayer unless we plan to pray."[11] I can tire of my prayers when it feels as though they fail to lift off the launching pad. A Facebook posting by Wesleyan scholar and renewal author Howard Snyder bolsters my faith: "Prayer is difficult because we are dealing with unseen forces and sometimes unseen results—or results that don't appear till much later."

Jesus taught we should always pray and not give up (see Luke 18:1). The discipline of prayer includes waiting for God to act. Not the type of waiting you do in a long line at Walmart or in a dentist's office. The Hebrew word for *wait* ("they who wait for the LORD shall renew their strength," Isaiah 40:31) is *qāwâ* and means "to trust and endure with hope and eager expectation, stretched as twisted strands of rope."[12] Here is the meaning: "I wait for the LORD, my soul waits, and in his word I hope" (Psalm 130:5). It is like waiting for your wedding day or for Spring.

If you have ever made direct appeals to someone, you understand how biblical prayer includes direct appeals to God. It is to "call upon the name of the Lord" (Genesis 4:26; Isaiah 12:4; Romans 10:11–13). It is to plead or praise God's personal presence by faith to deliver on His covenant promises, for those who need or affirm His intervention or salvation. Do you ever do that? Like this, "So Peter was kept in prison, but earnest prayer for him was made to God by the church" (Acts 12:5). Fervent, stretched out and straining prayer *was being made to God* for him.

Prayerlessness

Over the decades, I have observed and mourned that wholesale prayerlessness is pandemic, particularly in the Western Church. If prayer is the oxygen of the soul, would not planned prayer in the lives of Christians and churches be as essential as oxygen is for an intubated COVID-19 patient in an ICU? If the Bible contains over 600 prayers, in addition to the book of Psalms, which consists of another 150 prayers, would not that fuel our altars? Tim Keller writes, "Prayer is so great that wherever you look in the Bible, it's there. Why? Everywhere God is, prayer is."[13] Prayerlessness suffocates with no other options left for spiritual breath.

We offer routine prayer at our church services, at mealtimes and as we open and close meetings. But do we engage in cosmic combat with continuous, strenuous prayer, like "Epaphras . . . a servant of Christ Jesus, sends greetings. He is always wrestling in prayer for you, that you may stand firm in all the will of God, mature and fully assured" (Colossians 4:12 NIV)? We moan about life's clutter and clatter. We are frantic, weary and preoccupied. We have strenuous jobs. We are overwhelmed with all the unfinished tasks around the house. We grind through life and losses. Nevertheless, Paul insists, "Devote yourselves to prayer, being watchful and thankful" (Colossians 4:2 NIV).

Theological Shift

Abraham Heschel wrote, "The issue of prayer is not prayer; the issue of prayer is God."[14] In other words, the problem of prayer is theological, not practical. Our inattention to God and our independence from God cloud our search for God. The problem lies in our functional theology—lived theology. Søren Kierkegaard wrote, "As you have lived, so have you believed."[15]

When left unchecked, we can succumb to our inner atheist. There is a gravitational pull to live by humanistic unbelief without attention to God shown by meager prayer. And I question if deep down inside, we are not sure prayer works or God hears.

Theologian Donald Bloesch (echoing John Calvin) states, "Just as prayer is the cardinal evidence of faith, so prayerlessness is the salient hallmark of unbelief. Prayer is faith in action."[16]

A critical shift in my theology that lifted me out of this morass was to view prayer as communion and communication with God. It is my conscious relationship with God. Rather than show up on my terms with a list of hollow requests, like people who only contact you when they want something, I try to cultivate contemplative prayer with God. The word *contempla-*

tive comes from the Latin *con* ("with") and *templa* ("temple," God's dwelling place). Contemplative prayer aims to dwell with God as Christ dwells in us (see Ephesians 3:17).

The Physics of Prayer

Prayer can sparkplug supernatural energy into motion. Prayer from righteous people is potent. "The prayer of a righteous person has great power as it is working" (James 5:16). Let this truth motivate you. "The eyes of the Lord are on the righteous, and his ears are open to their prayer. But the face of the Lord is against those who do evil" (1 Peter 3:12). Prayer can release divine energy for healing and deliverance. It can plow through barricades of closed doors of resistant people to the Gospel (see Colossians 4:3). When fused with the proclaimed Gospel, devout prayer can help haul thousands of people into the Kingdom (see Acts 1:14; 2:14–47). Vigilant present-tense prayer is a steel-walled defense against temptation. "Watch and [continually] pray that you may not enter into temptation. The spirit indeed is willing, but the flesh is weak" (Mark 14:38).

Targeted prayer is *pāga*—the Hebrew word whose root is "to meet." It means to "encounter, entreat or strike upon."[17] It can refer to an intercessor—a go-between—who contacts God for others (see Jeremiah 27:18; Isaiah 59:16). Targeted prayer is spiritual lightning that strikes the mark with God's presence. "He covers his hands with the lightning and commands it to strike the mark [*pāga*]. Its crashing declares his presence" (Job 36:32–33). The physics of prayer resembles a ripple effect that activates lightning bolt impact.[18]

Our friends Frank and Kathy are devoted to *pāga*. When we visit, Frank prays for us. When we moved from Kelowna to Airdrie, Kathy knew Alberta winters were frigid. She made us a colorful polar fleece blanket. She tied 255 knotted tassels that border the entire blanket. Each tassel represents an intercessory prayer she offered to God for us while she made the blanket! Numerous times I have nestled inside that blanket when I needed literal and God's warmth. I also use it as a pillow when I lay prostrate in prayer on my office floor. May you blanket others in fervent prayer as a righteous person who can alter the weather (see James 5:17–18).

Practices of Presence-Centered Prayer

I invite you to practice presence-centered prayer. David McIntyre tells us:

> Firstly, it's necessary to realize the presence of God. The One who fills earth and heaven "is," in a singular and impressive sense, in the secret place. As the electric current in the atmosphere is concentrated in a lightning flash, so the presence of God becomes vivid and powerful in the prayer room.[19]

Here are three ways to stoke continual fire on the altar.

Talk to God

In his New York Times bestseller *The Untethered Soul*, Michael Singer addresses the mental dialogue of the nonstop voice we have in our head with our inner roommate—the conversations we have with *ourselves*. And some of what we say to ourselves is not even true! Tethered, we talk and listen to ourselves and adopt both sides of the conversation.

"I have a full day today. Don't know how I'll get through it. You shouldn't have scheduled so many meetings! Well, I should reschedule some. It's too late now. I'll never catch up. You're terrible."

I am learning to monitor the merry-go-round mental dialogue that revolves in my mind. I am learning to convert my thoughts into conversations with God—talk to God.

Although it is important and even indispensable for our spiritual lives to set apart time for God and God alone, our prayer can only become unceasing [prayer] when all our thoughts—beautiful or ugly, high or low, proud or shameful, sorrowful or joyful—can be thought in the presence of the One who dwells in us and surrounds us. By trying to do this, our unceasing thinking is converted into unceasing prayer, moving us from a self-centered monologue to a God-centered dialogue. To do this we want to try to convert our thoughts into conversation. The main question, therefore, is not so much what we think, but to whom we present our thoughts.[20]

I am learning to detect another voice in my head—God's. He might place thoughts, ideas, images, Scripture passages, impressions, insights or nudges that sometimes enter our minds and hearts through structured contemplation and reasoned analysis or through spontaneous bursts that pop in from nowhere. Missionary Frank Laubach knew how the mind works and journals how he talked and walked with God. Recorded in *Letters of a Modern Mystic*, this was his central practice: "My part is to live this hour in continuous inner conversation with God and in perfect responsiveness to his will."[21] Biblical prayers regularly directly address God with *you*.

That still small voice speaks within, easily undetected. God spoke to Nehemiah's heart (see Nehemiah 7:5), spoke through prophets and teachers during worship and fasting (see Acts 13:1–2), and spoke through the disciples' Spirit-guided deliberations (see Acts 15:28). Paul could distinguish his voice from the Lord's when he offered opinions to the Corinthians (see 1 Corinthians 7:10, 12). We have the mind of Christ (see 1 Corinthians 2:16). "All of the words that we are going to receive from God, no matter what may accompany them externally or internally," says Dallas Willard, "will ultimately pass through the form of our own thoughts and perceptions."[22] God seems to speak more in familiar than in fantastic ways.

113

As a mother who can detect her child's voice in a group of children, we can detect God's thoughts in our minds by practice and experience, familiarity and proximity of relationship. Scripture and the inner witness of the Spirit guide us.

Daily, I place myself in God's presence, meditate on His Word (see Psalm 1), devote myself to prayer being watchful and thankful (see Colossians 4:2), and pay attention to every spoken word (*rhēma*) that proceeds from God's mouth (see Matthew 4:4). Here is my routine. "O LORD, in the morning you hear my voice; in the morning I prepare a sacrifice for you and watch" (Psalm 5:3). I am usually up by 5:30 a.m. for at least ninety minutes to read Scripture, talk to God (pray), journal and watch.

Let's earnestly pray *to* God. "So Peter was kept in prison, but earnest prayer for him was made to God by the church" (Acts 12:5). And note Cornelius, a Roman commander of one hundred soldiers, "a devout, God-fearing man . . . [who] prayed regularly to God" (Acts 10:2 NLT). I love Mark Batterson's idea: "If you pray to God regularly, irregular things will happen on a regular basis."[23] Pray as if He is listening!

So, "Good morning, Lord! I have a full day today. Don't know how I'll get through it. I shouldn't have scheduled so many meetings! Are there any I should reschedule? Please fill me with Your Spirit, and may Your presence permeate my meetings. Guide my conversations today, that I'd be a blessing. Lord, I'll never catch up. Can You help me? Thanks for loving me."

I love the scenes in the movie *Fiddler on the Roof* where Tevye, the poor milkman with five daughters, talks with God about his undeserved poverty and his Russian traditions. He moans and muses and wrangles with God. Before I make decisions, do I inquire of the Lord as David did (see 1 Chronicles 14:8–16)? Do I ask God questions and wait for answers? Is prayer a two-way conversation or a one-way cell call where I talk and disconnect when I am done? The Bible supplies an avalanche of evidence of how God communicates directly with people and prophets. Like a radio station wavelength, we must tune into the wavelength of His voice.

Several years ago, I talked to God about my vision for mission and prayed He would open doors of opportunity for me to share the Word. As a district minister, I used Enterprise Car Rental. Because they picked me up and dropped me off, I had conversations with many staff members. An African fellow shared how his father was ill and faced death and he could not get over to see him. I had this impulse to ask if I could pray for him. As we sat parked in my driveway, I prayed for him, and through tears, he thanked me. The following week, I continued our conversation, shared the Gospel with him, and learned his dad had improved!

In another situation, I asked a female employee how she was feeling. She shared how demanding her job was and how she suffered from migraine headaches and could not sleep. I thought God wanted me to offer prayer. I chickened out. The following week on our way to my place, I asked her again how she was doing. Same reply. My heart began to pound. I knew God was nudging me. I told her I believed Jesus could heal and offered to pray for her.

She replied, "Well, I guess it couldn't hurt." I prayed for God to heal her migraines. Two weeks later, I asked how she was since I prayed for her. She replied, "Wow, the migraines are gone, and I can sleep!"

Vary Prayer Postures

We all have different personalities and preferences when it comes to styles of prayer. Silence and contemplative prayer appeal to some, while sound and celebration prayer appeal to others. Some relate to God from their minds and others from their senses. Some prefer to pray as they walk outside, while others prefer to pray in a den. Some enjoy public prayer while others do not. Some prefer spontaneity, others prefer structure.

There are multiple ways to practice presence-centered prayer. This includes the physicality of different prayer postures that can invigorate prayer. When our children were infants, my wife found it difficult to have any alone time or space to pray. So she would pray and quietly sing while she nursed and cuddled our little ones in our living room rocking chair in the serenity of the wee morning hours.

To keep me from mindless routines in prayer, I use different physical postures. The Bible offers an assortment of prayer postures. We can literally, and at times loudly, lift our voices, cry out, pour out our souls, lift our eyes, lift our hands, bow, kneel, prostrate themselves, walk, sit or stand to draw near to God, approach God's throne, seek God's face, and call upon the name of the Lord. There are tons of energetic and effective prayers in Scripture to learn from. The prayers of Psalms, Moses, Solomon, Jehoshaphat, Hezekiah, Nehemiah, Daniel, Jesus, Peter, Paul and the early Church offer endless varieties of God-centered, physical prayer.

I will sit in my office and pray with a Bible and journal. I pray both quietly and out loud. I will stand, lie prostrate or kneel on my office floor, walk outside and gaze into the sky. I crank up energetic live worship when I drive alone and absorb the sound of music. I convert the lyrics to contemplative or celebrative prayer and let my emotions and imagination soar!

While I lie in bed, my first act in the morning and my last act at night is to greet God. As I chat with people, I try to listen in stereo. I listen to people with my ears while I listen to the Spirit with my heart and mind. I pray as I preach and teach to ignite the spiritual gas the way a natural gas fireplace pilot light does, ready to ignite my communication with unction. I will also gesture with uplifted hands, voice and eyes, kneel or bow down. I asked Brian Stiller how I could inspire other leaders with prayer. His reply, "Make it majestic!"

Majestic prayer is caught more than taught.

Engage Scripture and Spirit

Here is a final practice for presence-centered prayer. When you read and pray from Scripture, you leverage God's Spirit-inspired words to you as your words back to Him. We engage Scripture and Spirit to infuse the content and direction of our prayers with God's truth and will. He is sure to listen. Have you ever noticed how a child can stonewall you with closed ears, though you might shout, "Listen to me!" But if you whisper, "Do you want some ice cream?" or "Would you like a movie night?" they are all ears! God is all ears when we pray His will (see 1 John 5:14).

As I read and pray from Scripture, the Spirit enlivens my heart to connect with God's presence. John Piper describes the interrelationship. "What I have seen is that those whose prayers are most saturated with Scripture are generally most fervent and most effective in prayer. And where the mind isn't brimming with the Bible, the heart is not generally brimming with prayer."[24] Let *Script*-ure script your prayer. Let the language of Scripture provide the language of prayer.

There is a drought of Scripture-fed and Spirit-led prayer today. Apply Jude's present tense appeal: "But you, beloved, building yourselves up in your most holy faith and praying in the Holy Spirit, keep yourselves in the love of God" (Jude 20–21). Let's become spiritual skyscrapers with our Scripture-fed most holy faith. Let's ascend to the upper room on the elevator of Spirit-led prayer. Andrew Murray states, "The connection between the prayer life and the Spirit life is close and indissoluble."[25]

The eternal flame of worship is prayer in God's house—spiritual sacrifices offered and mingled in song, liturgy, prayers, preaching and sacraments endowed by the Spirit's presence (see Psalm 116:17; Hebrews 13:15). Psalms capture this. Stanley Jaki suggests, "The purpose of the Psalms is to turn the soul into a sort of burning bush."[26]

And Isaiah 56:7 says, "These I will bring to my holy mountain, and make them joyful in my house of prayer; their burnt offerings and their sacrifices will be accepted on my altar; for my house shall be called a house of prayer for all peoples." Jesus cited the last sentence when He confronted the money changers at the Jerusalem temple (see Mark 11:17).

I prayed and marveled through two psalms per day for 75 days. Those 150 psalms inflamed my life of prayer! The Spirit seized my heart and transported me into an enchanted world teeming with praise and pleas that spotlight God's creative might, steadfast love and stately kingship. For starters, praise and pray through Psalm 138. Recently, I was in a Zoom prayer time when others prayed this psalm. It was thrilling! There is a YouTube video where you can view this sung version.[27]

We battle a devil and cosmic forces of evil that launch fiery missiles against us. As spiritual soldiers, let's daily wear our spiritual armor (see Ephesians 6:10–11). Paul teaches:

And take the helmet of salvation, and the sword of the Spirit, which is the word of God, praying at all times in the Spirit, with all prayer and supplication. To that end, keep alert with all perseverance, making supplication for all the saints.

Ephesians 6:17–18

The *word* of God here is the spoken word (*rhēma*). As we audibly speak out and pray God's Word (Scripture-fed), it fuels prayer directed and empowered by the Spirit (Spirit-led). At times, we must strive together—agonize—in our prayer to God for others from hostilities (see Romans 15:30).

Have you had times of private or public prayer where God's presence electrified its content and tone with laser clarity and propulsion? Scripture-fed and Spirit-led private and public prayer can focus presence-centered prayer. I have endured too many human-led prayer meetings that felt as hollow as a vacant rental property. I usually pray with an open Bible. I pray directly from strategic passages and personalize it. Here is an example:

> Rejoice always, pray without ceasing, give thanks in all circumstances; for this is the will of God in Christ Jesus for you. Do not quench the Spirit. Do not despise prophecies, but test everything; hold fast what is good. Abstain from every form of evil. Now may the God of peace himself sanctify you completely, and may your whole spirit and soul and body be kept blameless at the coming of our Lord Jesus Christ. He who calls you is faithful; he will surely do it.
>
> 1 Thessalonians 5:16–24

Lord Jesus, I choose to rejoice in Your goodness this morning. The joy of the Lord is my strength. May I pray without ceasing, without intermission, as I practice continual awareness of You today as we talk. Thank You, Lord, for my health, my family, my friends, my salvation, my ministry and the beauty of this day. May I be thankful in all circumstances I encounter. May I never extinguish the Spirit's fire in my life and leadership. Holy Spirit, have Your way. May I walk and live by Your empowering presence and power aglow with kāvôd. Fill me today.

Lord, I embrace the prophetic, and may I be a conduit of prophecy and Spirit-inspired words of strength, comfort and encouragement to others. Lord, help me practice Scriptural discernment to test what is good and discard what is not and avoid all evil in my life. God of peace, sanctify me wholly. Mark my life with Your holiness from the inside out, that I would be pure and blameless in my spirit, soul and body, wholly sanctified today. You are faithful and will surely do it.

Mark Buchanan concludes, "Beware little old ladies praying. Secretly they're revolutionaries who make Bolsheviks look like kindergartners. They comprise a veritable bomb-making factory. Pray the Psalms—offer your whole life before God. Pray without ceasing—bring your whole life into the presence of God. For now, it's incense. But one day . . . the fire will fall."[28] May we be living altars on which the fire of ceaseless prayer continually burns.

7

The Burning Heart

Presence-Centered Scripture Living

> They said to each other, "Did not our hearts burn within us while he talked to us on the road, while he opened to us the Scriptures?"
>
> Luke 24:32

With over 31,000 verses in the Bible, can you guess which Bible verse was the most cited worldwide in 2020—the year the COVID-19 pandemic began? In *Christianity Today*, Kate Shellnutt wrote:

> During the hardest moments of a particularly difficult year, Bible searches soared online, and a record number of people turned to Scripture for passages addressing fear, healing, and justice. The popular *YouVersion* Bible app saw searches increase by 80 percent in 2020, totaling nearly 600 million worldwide.

Here is the one verse that "ranked as the most searched, read, and bookmarked verse on the app: 'So do not fear, for I am with you; do not be dismayed, for I am your God. I will strengthen you and help you; I will uphold you with my righteous right hand'"[1] (Isaiah 41:10 NIV). This stellar verse spotlights the presence-centered life—"Don't fear, for I'm *with* you!"

Presence-Centered Scripture Learning

Scripture's purpose is to shape our thoughts about God, illumine reality and the Gospel, and train us in righteousness as it addresses our battered lives. Millions of people have paralyzing fear and crave emotional strength in these precarious times. Like an overprotective and smothering mother who frets that harm lurks everywhere for her children, chronic fear debilitates and governs how we view the world where everything is a potential threat. Life rockets multiple trials at us that require outside help. Here is the good news: God is as sovereign as He is relational. He is *with* us and promises strength and support. We need not fear. If we get our cues from ourselves or others or from CNN or Fox News rather than from God, we can careen into an abyss of discouragement and lose our way. There is another option: Read Scripture in the Emmaus way of the burning heart.

Read Scripture in the Emmaus Way of the Burning Heart

Famous people will write autobiographies and go on speaking tours to share their lives and commentaries on their books. I saw former United States President Barack Obama at the Saddledome in Calgary and later read his book *A Promised Land*. His book came alive because it reflected him as a person where I could hear his voice on each page. Imagine you are at a speaking tour of an Old Testament survey by Jesus. He takes you through the Scriptures with personal commentary about

Himself. They come alive as you hear His voice as God's Word on each page. Listen in:

> And beginning with Moses and all the Prophets, he interpreted to them in all the Scriptures the things concerning himself. So they drew near to the village to which they were going. He acted as if he were going farther, but they urged him strongly, saying, "Stay with us, for it is toward evening and the day is now far spent." So he went in to stay with them. When he was at table with them, he took the bread and blessed and broke it and gave it to them. And their eyes were opened, and they recognized him. And he vanished from their sight. They said to each other, "Did not our hearts burn within us while he talked to us on the road, while he opened to us the Scriptures?" . . . Then they told what had happened on the road, and how he was known to them in the breaking of the bread.
>
> Luke 24:27–32, 35

This passage about the disciples and Jesus on the road to Emmaus overflows with *kāvôd*. The resurrected Jesus offers an Old Testament survey to His doubting disciples. He draws them into a sacramental encounter of presence-centered Scripture learning. Jesus, the inconspicuous though central Old Testament character, opens their eyes to His presence then and now.

In his remarkable book *A More Christlike Word*,[2] Bradley Jersak develops a *Christotelic* reading of Scripture that reveals Christ as its goal or end (*telos*). The key for interpreting Scripture is to ask, "How does any given passage point to Christ and form Christlike people?"[3] While the Bible is the printed Word of God, Jesus is the living Word of God. He as the "the word of God is living and active, sharper than any two-edged sword. . . . And no creature is hidden from *his* sight, but all are naked and exposed to the *eyes of him* to whom we must give account" (Hebrews 4:12–13, emphasis added). This primarily refers to

Jesus, who is the *living* Word of God with all-seeing eyes, not to the Bible. And Jesus is also alive and active through Scripture.

Our goal is not to simply learn Scripture but to learn Christ, hear His voice and seek His penetrating presence. The apostles preached the Gospel directly from the Old Testament, where they applied its Christ-contained truths. We read Him *out of* the Old Testament not *into* it. He is woven within the story. You will detect Jesus in the books of the law, history, poetry and prophets.

Be warned. We can search Scripture but miss Jesus and life. "You search the Scriptures because you think that in them you have eternal life; and it is they that bear witness about me, yet you refuse to come to me that you may have life" (John 5:39–40). As the incarnate Word, Jesus generated illumination, presence and revelation. As He talked and opened Scripture (illumination), their hearts burned with fire (presence). As the Bread of Life, Jesus broke bread with them and their eyes opened (revelation). All sacramental encounters with the living Word.

The Pietists and Puritans taught that the Spirit must illuminate the meaning of Scripture seeded into a regenerate person's heart for it to bear the fruits of faith. This requires durable exegetical and experiential study to inform the mind and transform the heart to hear from God and practice presence-centered Scripture learning. Puritan Richard Sibbes remarks, "What the heart likes best, the mind studies most."[4]

As the operating system of life, the condition of our heart is the crucial factor for presence-centered Scripture learning. Scarce change occurs in us unless inspiration grips our hearts and drives our will. Jesus taught about four types of receptivity to the seed of God's Word to bear spiritual fruit in our life. Seed sown on unreceptive paths, rocks or thorns does not take root. The fourth type is receptive, "As for that in the good soil, they are those who, hearing the word, hold it fast in an honest and good heart, and bear fruit with patience" (Luke 8:15).

How is your heart? Is it open and receptive to Christ the Word? As a spiritual gardener, do you have patience for the seed of His Word to bear fruit in your life? If so, grip that Word in an honest and good heart. The verb is present tense—continue to hold and hang on to God's Word.

Engage Scripture

Nothing rivals the catalytic partnership of Scripture and Spirit immersed in prayer. "Take . . . the sword of the Spirit, which is the word of God, praying at all times in the Spirit" (Ephesians 6:17–18). Jesus proclaimed, "If you abide in my word, you are truly my disciples, and you will know the truth, and the truth will set you free" (John 8:31–32).

Here is my paraphrase: "If you dwell in Scripture, you are my genuine learners, and you will experience the truth that will liberate you." I daily read Scripture with prayer and seek God's presence. I dwell in the Bible and allow the Bible to dwell in my mind and heart. My passion matches what T. F. Torrance wrote about theologian Karl Barth, "For Barth, true Biblicism meant accustoming himself to breathe the air of divine revelation . . . and to indwell its message in such a way the truth of divine revelation became built into the very walls of his mind."[5]

To engage Scripture is to do so in transformational ways. My pattern is Psalm 1—the gateway into a life of prayer from the psalter:

> Blessed is the one who does not walk in step with the wicked or stand in the way that sinners take or sit in the company of mockers, but whose delight is in the law of the LORD, and who meditates on his law day and night. That person is like a tree planted by streams of water, which yields its fruit in season and whose leaf does not wither—whatever they do prospers.
>
> Psalm 1:1–3 NIV

When I was a student at Dallas Seminary, Dr. Howard Hendricks lodged a full moon image in my mind. He taught:

We can either be pipe or tree students of Scripture. A pipe is a conduit through which water flows from one end to the other. The water doesn't affect or change the pipe. A tree draws water into its roots from underground to nourish itself and produce leaves and fruit. The water affects and changes the tree. What are you? A pipe or a tree student of Scripture? Are you a conduit of Scripture, or does Scripture change you?

The key is to delight and meditate on the law—the Torah—the spiritual instruction of Scripture for life in Christ. He is the *telos*, goal, fulfillment of the law (see Romans 10:4). To delight is to enjoy and have passionate affection. I delight in Mexican food, dark roast coffee, theology, music, grandchildren and renewal. You may ask how do we meditate? Bill Johnson says, "If you've ever worried [or obsessed] about something, you already know how to meditate!"[6]

The Hebrew word for *meditate* is *hâgâh*. It means "to mutter, moan and muse."[7] One image is a lion who growls over his prey (see Isaiah 31:4). It also means to ponder, such as, "I will ponder all your work, and meditate on your mighty deeds" (Psalm 77:12). To meditate is to engage your mind in Scripture with delight, not empty it like Eastern mystics would or fill it with unspiritual ideas of a natural person (see 1 Corinthians 2:13–14). For a theological banquet on what it means to delight in and meditate on Scripture, growl over Psalm 119.

For a guided tour, use *How to Read the Bible Book by Book*.[8] For animated videos of Bible books, themes and podcasts, view *Bible Project*.[9] Someone quizzed British Baptist preacher Charles Spurgeon about how he defended the Bible. "'Very easy,' he responded. 'I defend the Bible the same way I defend a lion. I simply let it out of its cage!'"[10] And he said, "Visit many good books, but *live* in the Bible."[11] I have used Philip Reinders' *Seeking God's Face: Praying with the Bible through the Year*. It follows the Christian calendar with Bible readings and prayer. I also use the *YouVersion* Bible app. It is packed with helpful features.

Let's not read Scripture as a devotional self-help manual on how to live our Christian life or how to obey Jesus better by following laws. Read it to hear and obey God's voice. When God speaks, He activates spectacular results. The universe comes into existence or the dead come to life! God's Word, what He says, is a creative force. "God said, 'Let there be light,' and there was light" (Genesis 1:3). When God speaks by His Word, it triggers results. We read Scripture as the Gospel that announces the Good News of what Christ did and does, and what God promised and gives. God's Word does what it says, and God is what God does. When Jesus said to the paralytic, "Son, your sins are forgiven" and "Rise, pick up your bed, and go home," both occurred (Mark 2:5, 11).

Let me offer ways to engage Scripture for the presence-centered life.

I daily engage Scripture the first hour in the morning with a method called *P.R.O.P.* I explain this in my book *The Devout Life*, chapter 5, on "Transformational Use of Scripture."[12]

- *P* ray: Turn off all social media. Pick a quiet spot. Place yourself in the presence of God. Pray for the Spirit's illumination with a receptive heart. Pray the Scripture that you read.
- *R* ead: Read the text slowly and out loud. Enter the narratives. Note what the author is doing with the text and how it directs you to Christ. Read until God speaks.
- *O* bserve: Observe key terms, mood and main point. Observe metaphors and how they incite your imagination. Observe the theology: what it says about God, Spirit and Christ.

- *P* ractice: Personalize and practice the text in your beliefs and behaviors. Engage and live the text in how it shapes your life in Christlikeness. Meditate on the text.

I am encouraged that many millennial Christians are Bible readers,[13] though some might prefer an audio version. I recommend both. Remember, in oral societies where most people could not read and available manuscripts were scarce, ancient people had to hear Scripture read at the temple and synagogue and later in cathedrals and churches. Not until the invention of the printing press did we evolve into literary societies where the distribution of Bibles enabled individuals to read them.

For people to read the Bible in silence is a relatively modern practice. God made His Word public. The original monastic practice of *Lectio Divina* (divine reading) was usually accomplished out loud, not in silent reading. Listen to audio versions such as YouVersion and the Bible Gateway Audio Bible online. Let Scripture be the soundtrack of your life where you listen as you walk or drive, or use it in a group setting.

I will discuss the public reading of Scripture in chapter 9. But first, this verse: "So faith comes from *hearing*, and hearing through the word of Christ" (Romans 10:17, emphasis added). It does not say faith comes from *reading*. For faith to occur, we must hear. And the Word of Christ is *rhēma*—the spoken word. As Christ's Word is spoken audibly (see Romans 10:14–16) it activates faith. Let's hear Christ, the Word, as Scripture transmits His voice. In an abstract, text-based society, we need to hear the audible sound of Scripture that helps cultivate presence. And I will add, read and pray Scripture out loud in your private times, too.

Presence-Centered Scripture Living

In Scripture, Jesus makes the invisible God visible. God is Jesus-like. He is the radiance of God's glory (see Hebrews 1:3). We are a people of a person, not a people of a book, like Islam. And we do not simply read the dinner menu at The Keg spiritual steakhouse. We eat to enjoy the meal (see Psalm 34:8), which is Jesus the Bread of Life (see John 6:26–58). I love freshly baked sourdough bread with real butter. But God offers eternal bread from His bakery in heaven.

We eat it as we present tense keep on believing *into* Jesus (see John 6:35, 40, 47). We do not only believe *in* Jesus but believe *into* Him. We enter and abide as the Greek *eis* (into) shows throughout John. To believe *into* Jesus is like an unending journey into Narnia, not shut up in a wardrobe. Let's explore Aslan's enchanted country. Let's learn of and believe into Christ to become Christlike.

Experience Scripture

Jesus and James prod us to be doers of God's Word and not hearers only (see Luke 11:28; James 1:22). James corners us:

> For if anyone is a hearer of the word and not a doer, he is like a man who looks intently at his natural face in a mirror. For he looks at himself and goes away and at once forgets what he was like. But the one who looks into the perfect law, the law of liberty, and perseveres, being no hearer who forgets but a doer who acts, he will be blessed in his doing.
>
> James 1:23–25

Though we hear Scripture in sermons, that does not mean it is active in our lives. We can hear about diets and exercise and yet consume fattening food and skip the gym. Consider Pietist Johann Albrecht Bengel, who said, "Apply yourself wholly to the text; apply the text wholly to yourself."[14]

We can study Scripture as impersonal content or as personal communication from God. To get traction when you read the Bible, use the personal pronouns *I*, *me* and *my*. Take a passage such as 2 Corinthians 7:1 and make it "May I cleanse myself from every defilement of my body and spirit, as I bring my holiness to completion in my fear of God."

In group study, use the second person pronouns *we*, *us* and *our*: "Let us walk in a manner worthy of our calling . . . and be eager to maintain the unity of the Spirit in the bond of peace . . . as we were called to the one hope" (Ephesians 4:1–4).

It is easy to do flyovers in the abstract skies of ideas rather than land and live in them. In his book *A Secular Age*, Charles Taylor calls this an *ex*carnational faith—one that lives more in our head than in our heart, in our brain than in our body—opposite to *in*carnation.[15] It is entombed in Enlightenment rationalism. We can rattle around as the Tin Man did with no heart in *The Wizard of Oz*.

A philharmonic orchestra can only perform elegant music when the musicians perform and not merely read the score. For presence-centered Scripture living, we must not simply read Bible facts and theology but participate in them by obedience. A. W. Tozer writes, "At what point, then, does a theological fact become for the one who holds it a life-giving truth? *At the point where obedience begins.*" In that same book, he said, "Truth cannot aid us until we become participators in it. We only possess what we experience."[16]

After I taught my course on presence-centered spirituality and leadership at Ambrose Seminary, a group of students remarked they experienced some of what we discussed of God's manifest presence. Predictably, they confessed they did not have a theology for them. Together, we had "aha" moments. We explored how the Bible reports ways where God showed Himself to individuals and groups through genuine spiritual gifts, fillings, angels, visions and dreams, word and sacrament, healing and deliverance, miracles, signs and wonders, prophecy and revelation, physical phenomena, theophanies, audible voice and power encounters.

I love the account in Acts 4. It reports what occurred after those believers "lifted their voices together to God" and engaged in Scripture-fed, Spirit-led prayer for boldness and miracles (see Acts 4:23–30). "And when they had prayed, the place in which they were gathered together was shaken, and they were all filled with the Holy Spirit and continued to speak the word of God with boldness" (verse 31).

During the 1949–52 Scottish Hebrides revival, a similar event occurred in the village of Arnol, where a granite house shook during a prayer meeting inside. Revivalist Duncan Campbell reports:

> There are those in Arnol today who will bear witness to the fact that, while a brother prayed, the very house shook. I could only stand in silence as wave after wave of Divine power swept through the house, and in a matter of minutes following this heaven-sent visitation, men and women were on their faces in distress of soul.[17]

Rare but real!

Experience Scripture in Light of Pentecost

In his book *Spirit Hermeneutics*, Craig Keener argues all Christians should read Scripture from the vantage point of Pentecost. Not as Pentecostals per se, but as believers who live in the age of the Spirit that commenced in Acts 2. Prophecy, miracles, healing, visions, deliverance, powerful preaching, boldness, fervent prayer, gifts and fillings of the Spirit are repeatable experiences in Scripture since Pentecost. They convey God's manifest presence. Keener writes, "While careful study of Scripture helps counter the unbridled subjectivism of popular charismatic excesses, study that does not lead to living out biblical experience in the era of the Spirit misses the point of the biblical texts."[18]

Pastors will preach through the gospels and Acts. I have asked if they will simply preach or if they will actively practice them. One pastor, who preached through Matthew, confessed he felt nervous and never knew what to do when he came to healing or deliverance accounts. We do not see these daily, but biblical patterns show us what to expect.

When David writes, "Seek my face," I pray, "My heart says to you, 'Your face, LORD, do I seek'" (Psalm 27:8). When Luke reports "Jesus returned in the power of the Spirit to Galilee" (Luke 4:14), I pray for and seek to live in the Spirit's power. James advises, "Is anyone among you sick? Let him call for the elders of the church, and let them pray over him, anointing him with oil in the name of the Lord" (James 5:14). I carry a little metal vial with oil on my keychain, so I am ready to pray for the sick anytime, anywhere—at Tim Hortons, in living rooms, hospitals and churches. Like a method actor, I seek to internalize the script of *Script*-ure and act it!

Ever heard of method actors? These actors internalize their scripts and create the thoughts and feelings of their characters to enable lifelike performances. What could happen if we adopted a similar approach where Scripture enabled lifelike performances of its truths in our lives? What could happen if we abided in Jesus and walked as He walked (see 1 John 2:6)?

Go for the Glory

A few years ago in our meeting, I sat with my eight district board members in a nice room with comfy chairs at a church. Our usual routine was to share our personal stories and pray for each other for about ninety minutes before we launched into the agenda items for the day. One leader shared how he had developed some severe heart palpitations from stress. He sat sullen with an ashen face. I had a prod from the Lord to offer prayers of healing.

We gathered around him, and I took out my little vial and anointed his forehead with olive oil. We prayed with the laying-on-of-hands for about ten minutes and returned to our seats. I glanced at him and noticed his face literally glowed. He had a broad grin and bright eyes. The others sat stunned and smiled as they saw the same glow. A transformation occurred right before our eyes. He touched his chest and said his heart had calmed down. The room was dense with God's presence. We practiced James 5:14–15 in real time!

At our next meeting, he reported the palpitations had vanished and he did not need medication anymore, confirmed by his doctor. In September of 2021, he sensed the Lord encourage him to change his lifestyle to fast regularly, exercise and begin a low carb diet. He is now medication free from diabetes with low blood sugar and a strong heart. God can use a combination of supernatural and natural means to heal.

Have you ever heard of a metamorphosis? In the natural world, for example, it occurs when an unsightly cocoon transforms into an elegant butterfly. In the *Spirit*-ual world, it occurs when "we all, with unveiled face, beholding the glory of the Lord, are being transformed into the same image from one degree of glory to another. For this comes from the Lord who is the Spirit" (2 Corinthians 3:18). The verbs for beholding and being transformed are present tense and describe an ongoing process.

When we behold the Lord's glory face to face and gaze at Jesus, who mirrors God's radiant glory in the Gospel, a metamorphosis occurs. We become what we behold. Our entire being becomes increasingly radiant and elegant in Christlike glory from the Lord, the Spirit.

Continue to look at Jesus, and you will come to look like Him.

German composer and musician Johann Sebastian Bach affixed the letters SDG to the bottom of all his church scores and some of his secular ones. They refer to the Latin *Soli Deo Gloria*: "To God alone be glory." What is affixed to the bottom of your life and mine? Let's go for the glory, with presence-centered Scripture living.

8

Fruitful Union

Presence-Centered Discipleship

The church in North America is dramatically overpro-
grammed and underdiscipled. Are we making disciples
or faking them?

Will Mancini[1]

On September 16, 1985, scorched by in-house turmoil, Steve
Jobs exited the company he founded in 1976—Apple Inc. Twelve
years later, in 1997, he returned as Apple's interim CEO on the
identical date of September 16. With the company near the edge
of the grave, Steve Jobs set out to reengineer Apple. He searched
for a new advertising agency that could help prove to the world
Apple was alive. He hired Chiat/Day, whose creative director,
Craig Tanimoto, designed a series of black and white images
of revolutionary people and events. On each image was the
rainbow-colored Apple logo and the words "Think Different."

Within twelve months the "Think Different" advertising campaign rejuvenated Apple, and its stock price tripled.

There was some debate over the grammatical use of the noun *different* rather than the adverb *differently*. Jobs insisted on think different as in think victory or think big. The slogan stood out and drove the point. Steve Jobs' searing personality and ferocious drive ignited world-changing creativity within his engineering teams. In 2011, when he died of pancreatic cancer at age 56, Apple had become the world's most valuable company that revolutionized computers, music, animated movies, cell phones, tablets and digital publishing. He pioneered "Think Different"[2] with his vision "to put a ding in the universe."[3]

Think Different Discipleship

Most Christians would agree discipleship is essential for spiritual growth. Dallas Willard says, "The word 'disciple' occurs 269 times in the New Testament." But churches have not made discipleship a condition of being a Christian or of membership. "Churches are filled with 'undiscipled disciples.' . . . Most problems in contemporary churches can be explained by the fact that members have never decided to follow Christ."[4] He calls this the great *omission*.

The term *discipleship* is often used generically as the Christian life. When I use the term, it refers to how to be and make followers of Jesus as Lord. Disciples followed rabbis. As apprentice learners, they did not sit in classroom lectures, but learned their rabbi's lifestyle and teaching as they observed, lived with and followed them. Let's make disciples who make disciples who follow Jesus as the heart and not a part of church mission.

Let's "think different" discipleship.

For many, discipleship means to follow a program, listen to preaching and podcasts and do Bible studies—transfer information about discipleship into our heads. These are all overrated and overused, especially in the West. Do we assume transformation will occur if we expose people to enough information? Scores of people soldier through studies and worship services year after year with minor signs of improvement. Me included.

If the Spirit's anointing (divine influence) electrifies it, the truth can activate a heart response for change when mingled with repentance. But Reggie McNeal states, "We have very little evidence that academic or conferential learning changes behavior."[5] We practice disciple-making in real time together, when we observe it lived out on mission with Jesus. Not simply studied as information but as imitation.

On Mission with Jesus

When important dignitaries make pronouncements, throngs of reporters and people take notice with ears glued to their words. When Warren Buffett delivers investment opinions, the markets buzz with notice. Jesus opened an earth-to-Kingdom window into His pronouncement priorities:

> And Jesus came and said to them, "All authority in heaven and on earth has been given to me. Go therefore and make disciples of all nations, baptizing them in the name of the Father and of the Son and of the Holy Spirit, teaching them to observe all that I have commanded you. And behold, I am with you always, to the end of the age."
>
> Matthew 28:18–20

If Jesus stacked His supreme authority behind this commission, you would think we had better beeline it to the front and get on board. Will Mancini muses, "The functional Great Commission in North American churches has become: Go into all the world and make more worship attenders, baptizing them in the name of small groups and teaching them to volunteer a few hours a month."[6]

Jesus delegated His Gospel mission to His followers. If you check Twitter's top ten accounts, you will discover who people obsessively follow. In September 2022, millions followed Barack Obama, Justin Bieber, Katy Perry, Elon Musk, Cristiano Ronaldo and Taylor Swift. Presence-centered discipleship—our co-mission—is Jesus on His mission with us. He is not holed up at the head office but in the field alongside us. If there is no mission, is there discipleship?

Many Christians get their cues more from culture through social media and political ideology than through *catechesis*—the teaching of Jesus and the Bible. In *The Atlantic*, Peter Wehner cites James Ernst of Eerdmans publishers: "What we're seeing is massive discipleship failure caused by massive catechesis failure. . . . The evangelical Church in the US over the last five decades has failed to form its adherents into disciples. So there is a great hollowness."[7]

Cable news and social media feeds can disciple Christians more than Christ does. The Netflix documentary *The Social Dilemma* offers a dark view into the ghastly potential. Henri Nouwen offers a counter missional practice: "The farther the outward journey takes you, the deeper the inward journey must be. Only when your roots are deep can your fruits be abundant."[8]

Think Abide in Jesus

Matthew 28 gets heaps of airtime in the evangelism and discipleship world. A staccato cadence orchestrates its theology and practices: "Go and make followers of all people groups; baptize them and teach them to obey Me; I'm with you to the end."

Here is a think different discipleship paradigm: Jesus used Palestinian vineyards and Israel as God's vineyard (see Isaiah 5:1–6) to teach a discipleship lesson. He is the true vine, the Father is the gardener, and we are the branches. We cannot bear grapes on our own. Detached from Jesus, we can do zero (see John 15:1–5). Practice think different discipleship. "If you abide in me, and my words abide in you, ask whatever you wish, and it will be done for you. By this my Father is glorified, that you bear much fruit and so prove to be my disciples" (John 15:7–8). Three simple words contain Olympic gold medal potential for discipleship: *abide in me*—live, lodge, remain in Jesus. Just as we live in our homes, we must live in Christ—in dynamic real time union with Him. Stay attached and receive from Him. Detached branches wither and die.

The proof is in the practice. Only those who stay attached as branches to Jesus the vine bear much spiritual fruit with succulent lives "filled with the fruit of righteousness that comes through Jesus Christ, to the glory and praise of God" (Philippians 1:11). To *abide* means to dwell or make our home in Jesus. Just as the Father abides or dwells in Jesus (see John 14:10) and the Spirit dwells in us (see John 14:17) we must abide in dependent connection to Jesus. This is the key to spiritual formation and discipleship.

I always advise students and church leaders to teach their people how to abide in Jesus and bear much fruit. We can abide in other things: our anger, our ambition, our pain, our job. But let's co-reside with Jesus. "Abide in me, and I in you" (John 15:4). What is in Jesus flows into us through the living sap of the Spirit's indwelling presence.

After Jesus promised He would manifest Himself to us (see John 14:21), "Judas (not Iscariot) said to him, 'Lord, how is it that you will manifest yourself to us?'" (John 14:22). His answer is astounding. "If anyone loves me, he will keep my word, and my Father will love him, and we will come to him and make our home with him" (John 14:23). While Jesus went to prepare a future home or dwelling place (*monē*) in heaven for us (see John 14:2), He and His Father come to make their present home (*monē*) in us. This echoes God's Old Testament promise to *dwell* with His people (see Leviticus 26:11–12; Ezekiel 37:27–28). Imagine that your landlord or banker moves in to live with you! Jesus moves in to live with us along with the Father and the indwelling Spirit and manifests Himself to us. So, the Godhead is a homebody!

Bear Fruit in Jesus

For think different discipleship, I teach through John 15:7–8 and show photos of world-class vineyards in the Okanagan Valley, where we lived. I ask, "If we don't consistently bear *much fruit* in our lives (present tense) are we disciples? Do our lives bring glory to the Father?"

And how is our prayer life? We cannot produce fruit. We can only bear fruit. It is a natural organic result that occurs over time when we stay in a life-giving relationship with Jesus Christ. Think of a well-manicured French vineyard with world-class love, joy, peace, patience, kindness, goodness, faithfulness, gentleness and self-control hanging from your life (see Galatians 5:22).

I grew up in Southern California near Orange County—home of Disneyland, Knott's Berry Farm and 150 miles of sun-baked beaches. Until urban expansion, Southern California was a patchwork of orchards and groves: orange, lemon, grapefruit, peach, walnut and avocado. As a boy, I played in many orchards and picked those fruits to revel in taste-dazzling fruit. That is how Orange County and Garden Grove got their names.

Garden Grove has the highest number of churches per capita in California. Orange County produced Christian leaders such as Charles Swindoll, John Wimber, Greg Laurie, Todd Hunter and Rick Warren. It is a county full of faith and fruit. If there is not much fruit, is there discipleship?

Presence-Centered Practices

Presence-centered discipleship is missional spirituality that feeds and forms mission. I have led cluster groups to disciple pastors and men's groups where I did this: "And what you have heard from me in the presence of many witnesses entrust to faithful men, who will be able to teach others also" (2 Timothy 2:2). I also did this in colleges of piety (Pietist discipleship groups) similar to what John Wesley did with his house church class meetings that fueled and sustained Methodist renewal for decades. I have also used *TIE* groups—*Three Is Enough*.

Todd Hunter offers this simple model you might adapt to foster discipleship in community. It means three friends or colleagues who do three practices. The *TIE* groups function in places of daily life—the workplace, school, home or coffee shop. *Three Is Enough* groups travel the inward journey of spiritual formation and the outward journey of serving others. You meet weekly or biweekly for sixty minutes (for breakfast, lunch or coffee) with two other friends or colleagues, in person or online.[9] Here is the format:

1. Read Scripture and share your reflections with the goal to live them.
2. Pray for alertness to the Spirit's guidance and pray for each other and others.
3. Serve others by being alert, by noticing others, as an expression of mission together.

When I was pastor of discipleship at Vernon Alliance Church, BC, I taught a course on lifestyle discipleship. As our primary curriculum, we compiled all the commands of Jesus recorded in Matthew's gospel. I distributed the five-page document and said, "OK, now let's go and obey them!" When I served as the district minister for the Baptist General Conference in Alberta, my first goal was to develop a new mission statement with our 29 churches. We settled on "Help equip and empower missional disciple-making leaders and churches in Alberta." We saw tangible results in the practice of presence-centered missional discipleship.

One goal I have is to equip disciples in wholesome feeding habits for holiness.

The story goes that one evening, an old Cherokee told his grandson about a battle that goes on inside people.

He said, "My son, the battle is between two wolves inside us all. One is Evil: anger, envy, jealousy, sorrow, regret, greed, arrogance, self-pity, guilt, resentment, inferiority, lies, false pride, superiority and ego. The other is Good: joy, peace, love, hope, serenity, humility, kindness, benevolence, empathy, generosity, truth, compassion and faith."

The grandson thought about it for a minute and then asked his grandfather: "Which wolf wins?"

The old Cherokee simply replied, "The one you feed."

Word-Centered Prayer

Here is the first of two practices for presence-centered discipleship: *word-centered prayer*. Jesus taught, "If you make yourselves at home with me and my words are at home in you, you can be sure that whatever you ask will be listened to and acted upon" (John 15:7 MSG). Spoken words shape our minds through television, radio and social media. What Jesus says, not only said, must shape our prayer. As an athlete who is locked into the zone, Jesus locked into continuous prayer with the Father (see John 12:49).

When Jesus built his church, He built a praying church. What kind of church are you building? When Jesus made disciples, he made praying disciples. What kind of disciples are you making? The size of your prayer life determines the size and scope of your ministry.[10]

Jesus promised, "If you abide in me, and my words [*rhēmata*] abide in you, ask whatever you wish, and it will be done for

141

you" (John 15:7). This is quite the promise! As you abide and ask, it generates answered prayer!

The content of God's fixed *written* words as Scripture is *logos*. The content of God's *spoken* words can be *logos* or *rhēma*, but *rhēma* words are never used of written words, only of spoken words. The *logos* often refers to the Gospel message (see Acts 4:4; 10:44). God can speak through *logos* and *rhēma* as we read Scripture, pray, are open to prophecy and practice God awareness as we walk, drive, work and go about our day. The words of parents, teachers and influencers tend to dwell in us.

I remember my stepdad's words: "Never lie, because you'll have to remember what you said." Jesus declared, "It is the Spirit who gives life; the flesh is no help at all. The words [*rhēmata*] that I have spoken to you are spirit and life" (John 6:63).

Jesus said, "Man shall not live by bread alone, but by every word [*rhēma*] that comes from the mouth of God" (Matthew 4:4). The Greek verb *comes from* (or proceeds) is *ekporeuomenō*. It depicts speech that continually comes out from God's mouth. It is present tense to denote a continuous reality—God's *now* words.[11] We live on every word God speaks to us in real time— whether it is about our job, parenting, finances, spiritual life, relationships or direction. "It takes more than bread to stay alive. It takes a steady stream of words from God's mouth" (Matthew 4:4 MSG).

Jesus said, "My sheep hear my voice, and I know them, and they follow me" (John 10:27). Jesus speaks to His sheep, and they *follow* Him as disciples should. Most churches and theological schools do not train disciples how to hear His voice except the traditional "Jesus speaks through Scripture." Jesus speaks, but are we tuned in? "God speaks in one way, and in two, though man does not perceive it" (Job 33:14). Like a radio station, we must tune in to the wavelength of His voice. We can listen in stereo through Scripture and the Spirit.

Scripture shows multiple ways that God communicates. He can place words directly into our minds through prophecy, visions, dreams, revelation, preaching, teaching, prayer, worship, impressions, word pictures, emotions, the senses, visitations, audible voice and the inner witness of the Spirit. Have you ever read the Bible, listened to a sermon, been in prayer or worship, had a dream, an impression or nudge, a flash of insight or an impulse, or had a word shared with you in which God spoke to you? Or have you ever prayed God would speak through a preacher or a teacher? God's *rhēma* was probably transmitted. Richard Foster remarks:

> The Holy Spirit moves among his people in the Prayer of the Heart. Perhaps the most common way of all is through special revelatory impressions and words that the Spirit imparts to the individual. This is often called a *rhema*, Greek meaning simply "word." . . . this "quickening of the Word" encourages us that God is near and deeply interested in the particular circumstances of our lives. A special *rhema* also comes to us frequently from other people, in which divine revelation from God is applied to the specifics of our lives.[12]

Suppose God bound Himself only to use the Bible when He speaks to people. That would pose an insurmountable problem for those who do not have a Bible, cannot read or do not read the Bible. The Bible reports how God spoke directly or by the Spirit to scores of people who were not reading Scripture at the time. Can Jesus speak to you without your Bible? He can speak through the fixed Word *of* the Lord and dynamic words *from* the Lord. The book of Acts shows this.

Jesus announced, "You did not choose me, but I chose you and appointed you that you should go and bear fruit and that your fruit should abide, so that whatever you ask the Father in my name, he may give it to you" (John 15:16). Jesus directly hand-picked and selected us to bear fruit that abides so that the

Father will grant our prayers. How? We will be in such close communion with Him that our asks will fit His will, in Jesus' name. Children who know their mother's will submit their asks that fit her will. God's fruitful children will do the same with the Father. We will also leverage Jesus' name—His reputation and authority—in ways we would leverage someone's name for an endorsement or reference. Children also leverage mom's name in their appeals to dad!

With a magnetic pull, God drew me into a pursuit of His presence. As I jumped into study, God spoke to me through Psalm 105:4. It lanced my heart. "Seek the LORD and his strength; seek his presence continually!" I prayed this and other passages on God's presence and glory. He lodged the word *kāvôd* into my mind and invited me into more detailed study. Daily, I prayed I would experience and host God's presence.

Every chance I got, I taught and preached on God's presence, and I prayed for His presence to permeate my live meetings, my Zoom meetings and my conversations with people. People remarked how they felt the weight of His presence. Different people invited me to share my journey from pagan to presence in person and on Zoom. I detected the Lord leading me to teach a course and seminar, which I have a few times. The results were identical—students encountered *kāvôd*.

One Sunday before I preached, I met with the associate pastor in his office. Before the service, as we prayed together, he shared a couple of prophetic words. He believed there was a book to come from me. He was unaware that two months earlier, the Lord had downloaded a vision into my heart for this book you are now reading.

Obedience to Jesus

The late David Yonggi Cho pastored the world's largest church in Seoul, South Korea, that claimed 750,000 members. Years ago, pastor Larry Lea asked him, "'Dr. Cho, how did you build such a great church?' He smiled back at me and, with no hesitation, replied, 'I pray, and I obey.'"[13]

The second core practice for presence-centered discipleship and the key to abiding in Jesus is *obedience*. Jesus continues, "As the Father has loved me, so have I loved you. Abide in my love. If you keep my commandments, you will abide in my love, just as I have kept my Father's commandments and abide in his love" (John 15:9–10).

We are information-oriented rather than obedience-oriented in our discipleship. But Jesus promised, "If you abide in my word, you are truly my disciples, and you will know the truth, and the truth will set you free" (John 8:31–32). To abide is to obey. To know truth is to live it. A revolution of revelation erupted in me when I discovered "As the Father has loved me, so have I loved you. Abide in my love" (John 15:9).

When I teach discipleship from John 15, I pause at this verse and ask, "How much does the Father love Jesus?" After thoughtful reflection, people land on "infinitely." I ask, "So how much does Jesus love us?" They get the logic and reply, "Jesus loves us infinitely!" I have watched that truth penetrate people's hearts where they stare in awe. Personally, it blows me away because I never felt loved as a kid. I ask, "How do we dwell in Jesus' love?" The passage teaches us that it is through obedience (see verse 10). Jesus dwelt in the Father's love the same way.

When children or grandchildren experience unconditional love with smiles, hugs and positive words spoken with grace, they thrive and want to dwell in it. Obedience flows more naturally from their response to love rather than that imposed from an angry parent through force or punishment who barks, "Because I said so!" When we say, "Listen to me," we mean "Obey me."

The word *obedience* comes from the Latin, "listening." When God appeared to Solomon in a dream and asked him what he wanted, Solomon replied, "Give your servant therefore an understanding mind to govern your people" (1 Kings 3:9). The Hebrew is a listening heart or an obedient heart. Only those who truly hear truly obey, from the heart.

During the transfiguration of Jesus, God's glory overshadowed the disciples in a bright cloud. He announced, "This is my beloved Son, with whom I am well pleased; listen to him" (Matthew 17:5). I love Neil Cole and *Starling Initiatives'* mission to catalyze Kingdom movements. Their simple plan is "Listen to Jesus and do what He says."[14]

The word *obedience* can suggest old-fashioned ideas of duty, rules or compliance. For those who value their independence, obedience can feel like a ball and chain. But it is an exercise of faith. Faith activates obedience (see Romans 1:5) and is an antidote to evil desires (see 1 Peter 1:14 NIV). Dietrich Bonhoeffer wrote, "Only he who believes is obedient, and only he who is obedient believes. . . . Faith only becomes faith in the act of obedience."[15]

Children chafe at obedience and resist restrictions. If left to themselves, they can morph into *Lord of the Flies* monsters who self-govern into catastrophe. Obedience is the concrete foundation of lifestyle discipleship. Years ago, a man offered to pay me ten dollars per hour as his pastor to meet each week at a nearby Tim Hortons and teach him how to study the Bible.

I agreed to meet with him but said, "Give the money to the food bank. You need to obey Jesus and do what the Bible teaches."

His reply, "That's easy for you to say, you get paid to obey Jesus!"

In *Renovation of the Heart*, Dallas Willard wrote,

The idea that you can trust Christ and not intend to obey him is an illusion generated by the prevalence of an unbelieving "Christian culture." In fact, you can no more trust Jesus and not intend to obey him than you could trust your doctor and your auto mechanic and not intend to follow their advice. If you don't intend to follow their advice, you simply don't trust them.[16]

Is there discipleship without obedience? Jesus corners us: "Why do you call me 'Lord, Lord,' and not do what I tell you?" (Luke 6:46).

Jesus declares the purpose of presence-centered discipleship: "These things I have spoken to you, that my joy may be in you, and that your joy may be full" (John 15:11). Just as vintage wine can gladden your heart (see Psalm 104:15), vintage discipleship can fill you with joy. Perhaps something to "think different" about.

PART 3

HOSTING GOD'S PRESENCE

9

The Habitation of *Kāvôd*

Presence-Centered Churches

The low view of God entertained almost universally among Christians is the cause of a hundred lesser evils everywhere among us. . . . With our loss of the sense of majesty has come the further loss of religious awe and consciousness of the divine Presence.[1]

I love the Church. As a pastoral leader, I have camped on the green parklands of the Vineyard, Mennonite Brethren, Christian and Missionary Alliance, and Baptist traditions with one ardent passion—to kindle the spiritual renewal of Christians and churches to flourish in missional disciple-making. In our polarized world, let's engage culture as the sons "from Issachar, men who understood the times and knew what Israel should do" (1 Chronicles 12:32 NIV). What should we do?

It starts with two questions. What is the Church's future, and what keeps you in your church? In his book *Future Church*, Will Mancini identifies the four most common reasons people attach to a church:

1. Place—people like the facility
2. Personality—people like the pastor
3. Programs—people like the activities
4. People—people like the people

This may be oversimplified, but he nails it, and there are combinations of these. He suggests the "lower room" of a church's provision houses these attachments and church staff spend considerable time there. But he questions whether it produces disciples and *real* church growth? His alternative is to add an "upper room" that houses the church's unique call and disciple-making vision.[2]

There is much to commend Mancini. It is my observation, however, that many churches lack spiritual vitality and growth because they lack God's presence in an "upper room." Their centers are place, personality, programs, people or purpose, but not presence! The Barna Group reports:

Most people (66 percent) feel they've had "a real and personal connection" with God while attending church. However, that means one-third of those who have attended a church in the past have never felt God's presence while in a church setting. Also, when asked about frequency, most of those who have attended church describe these encounters as rare.[3]

In addition, of the 30,000 churches in Canada and 380,000 in the United States, 80–85 percent are either plateaued or in decline. In research that spans 25 years with 2.3 million people, 75,000 churches, in 86 countries, Christian Schwarz of *Natural Church Development* concludes, "Research indicates, on average, the longer someone is a Christian, the more likely they will regress in their Christian journey."[4] He argues this reveals a dramatic decrease in the quality of their prayer experience, the transforming influences of faith and the positive influence worship services had on them. And this is largely from a resistance to change, a static concept of Christianity and a focus on organizational versus individual levels in church change processes.

Schwarz notes that believers and unbelievers (particularly Millennials) crave God's transcendent, transforming presence in daily life. He states we must reclaim the New Testament reality of God's *energy* as a key to spiritual transformation. We should translate the Greek word *energeia* not as "working" or "activity" but as "energy" in Ephesians 1:19 and 4:16, in 1 Corinthians 12:6 and in James 5:16—God's transcendent, eternal and divine reality expressed in real time.[5]

If the lower and upper rooms do not house God's presence and energy, we might build renovated show homes rather than habitations of *kāvôd*—lovely fireplaces without fire.

Crisis reveals and clarifies. During COVID-19, numerous church leaders discovered their connection was more to their methods than to mission. And our culture did not view the Church as an essential service. Some thought the pandemic would force the Church in new directions. It did. It stirred more prayer, soul care, the use of social media and virtual teams, and innovation for an outward focus and mental health. It spawned hybrid online and in-person church and digital discipleship.

But after two grueling years, when post-pandemic relief was in sight, Russian President Putin brutally invaded Ukraine. The globe quaked from the impact not seen since World War II. My heart sank and my mind reeled as anxiety churned in me. I had to refrain from overexposing myself to alarming cable news and disinformation, and I had to hang on tighter to King Jesus, the truth of Scripture, prayer and God's presence. Most pre- and post-pandemic churches and seminaries today are ill-equipped to lead in this new world of relentless volcanic upheaval.

Presence-centered churches are the Church's future.

What is the strongest gravitational attraction churches can offer? What drew throngs of people to the early Church? Was it not God's manifest presence? Churches should offer mission-focused programs with noble preaching and worship. But not as the center. If they lack God's presence, they will exhaust enormous energy delivering temple goods and services with no deity in them. They risk becoming like Ichabod, where God's glory (*kāvôd*) departed from Israel (see 1 Samuel 4:21). Church gatherings must be places to encounter God and not simply to expound God.

What Is the Church?

What is the Church? A building or a place? No, it is a people of the presence. A church exists where a group of Christ-followers corporately function as the Body of Christ, the royal priesthood, the household of God, the bride of Christ and the temple of the Spirit to fulfill Christ's mission to proclaim and practice the Gospel and make disciples. A habitation of *kāvôd*.

Habitation of Kāvôd

A central biblical metaphor for the Church is God's temple (see 1 Corinthians 3:16). It is a spiritual house built with living stones (see 1 Peter 2:4–5). This temple houses God's manifest presence by the Spirit as His dwelling place or habitation. Paul writes:

> For through him we both have access in one Spirit to the Father. So then you are no longer strangers and aliens, but you are fellow citizens with the saints and members of the household of God, built on the foundation of the apostles and prophets,

Christ Jesus himself being the cornerstone, in whom the whole
structure, being joined together, grows into a holy temple in the
Lord. In him you also are being built together into a dwelling
place for God by the Spirit.

Ephesians 2:18–22

God ordains us as His family household members to serve
as temple priests, prophets, musicians, preachers, pastors and
other spiritually gifted citizens of heaven to offer prayer and
praise as a holy nation—a house of prayer for all nations—a
habitation of *kāvôd*.

Imagine you and your church are houses of holy fire where
guys and gals, young and old, gather as coequal spiritual priests
to seek God's face in worship. As you gather, the spiritual com-
bustion ignites an inferno of God's blazing presence on par
with John Wesley's report:

After preaching to an earnest congregation at Coleford, I met
the Society. They contained themselves pretty well during the
exhortation, but when I began to pray the flame broke out:
many cried aloud; many sunk to the ground; many trembled
exceedingly, but all seemed to be quite athirst for God and pen-
etrated by the presence of his power.[6]

What if we designed our church gatherings as houses of
prayer and presence where God's *kāvôd* breaks out to burn
continually, where He is so near and vivid that we flourish in
an environment of sublime encounter? Duvall and Hays stoke
my imagination for the possibilities:

At the heart of this connection [to Eden] is the presence of God,
for it is the "presence" or the "indwelling" of God that defines
what a temple is . . . temples were regarded as the residences
of the gods and not simply as gathering places for worship, as
churches often are viewed today.[7]

It is a sacred place that houses a deity.

155

Hosting God's Presence

I have been in thousands of church and conference gatherings. Hundreds stand out as Jacob-style Bethels where the Spirit's tangible nearness was so concentrated that a hushed tranquility that defies explanation dominated. After the worship set concluded in a Prairie College chapel service where I was to preach, I could barely walk or talk. Dazed by *kāvôd*, tears welled up in my eyes as I approached and stood at the podium. After I regained my composure, I offered my sermon.

God's presence pulsates with immaculate radiance that can transfix you with His penetrating holiness mingled with electrifying joy. I have witnessed baptism services where people put their faith in Jesus on the spot and jumped into the tank fully clothed! I have worshiped in services where the music so enthroned the Lord upon our praises (see Psalm 22:3) that the worship team and congregation stood in weightless timelessness, drenched in waves of holiness, unable to move or sing, transported on unplanned excursions.

I have listened to sermons that pierced my heart and to Scripture readings that enthralled my mind to the point that my skin buzzed and my heart raced. I have sat awestruck during the Eucharist as the sacramental elements electrified our awareness of Christ, who occupied the room.

For Evangelicals especially, what is the center of our gatherings: preaching or presence? Bill Johnson offers a challenge:

> Somewhere in church history, the focus of our corporate gatherings became the sermon. This is not to devalue the Scriptures. Israel camped around the tabernacle of Moses, which housed the Ark of the Covenant. This was the absolute center of life for the nation. Israel camped around the Presence of God, while the church often camps around a sermon. Being Presence-centered as a church, a family, and as individuals must be put on the front burner again.[8]

Prayer and Preparation

My wife is a social expert and host. Before we have guests over for dinner, she leads. I help prepare our home to bless our guests. We tidy the living room, clean the bathroom, set the table, prepare the meal, light vanilla candles and stoke the fireplace if it is winter. We get ready to welcome our guests and offer them warm fellowship and tasty food. She sets the mood. The guests also come prepared to enjoy the meal and our company. The key to the dinner is the conversation and communion that creates a relational presence between hosts and guests.

Imagine a church that hosts God's presence for its guests—the members and attenders. The leaders responsible for the gatherings prepare the meal and the ambiance for the guests to taste and see the Lord's good (see Psalm 34:8), to come into His presence with singing and into His courts with praise (see Psalm 100). The primary way to prepare the habitation to host God's presence is through prayer. The model is Mary, who is seated at the feet of Jesus rather than Martha, who is stressed and standing in the kitchen. God does not call His habitation a house of preaching or a house of worship. Those occur there. He calls it a house of prayer for all nations (see Mark 11:17).

The guests also come prepared to enjoy the meal and fellowship. They practice holy habits in their personal lives at home to fuel their spiritual formation and passion for God. They are not slothful in zeal but are fervent in spirit (ablaze with the Spirit) serving the Lord; they rejoice in hope, are patient in affliction and faithful in prayer (see Romans 12:11–12). As communication and communion are linked, so are prayer and presence.

Unfortunately, few churches and guests arrive prepared in prayer, and most churches offer minimal prayer during their gatherings. They often rely solely on the Word and worship for the meal. Like engaging conversation, prayer is the leading way to communicate and commune with God. Most women know how to host guests for dinner, and in my experience, they are often the ones who pray the most.

The Flourishing Congregations Institute at Ambrose University presented their national survey results.[9] They asked 8,110 respondents what the top six most important parish/congregational life elements impacted their spiritual life/discipleship. Here is the ranking:

1. Preaching/teaching (68%)
2. Music/singing (45%)
3. Eucharist/communion (35%)
4. Volunteering in church (26%)
5. Prayer (17%)
6. Small groups (16%)

It is that telling that prayer ranked fifth in importance for spiritual life, slightly above small groups. How much is prayer chief in our worship services, board meetings, ministries and personal lives? Is prayer as central as preaching and worship? What about the time we expend plowing through jam-packed agendas? Tommy Barnett of Phoenix First Assembly of God remarked, "The presence of God in the midst of a church is directly proportional to the amount of prayer that takes place there."[10]

Scripture, Spirit, Sacrament

In broad categories, Evangelicals are Scripture-centered, Pentecostals are Spirit-centered, and Liturgicals are Sacrament-centered. The Scripture portrays God's presence, the Spirit manifests God's presence and the Eucharist (and Baptism) mediates God's presence. I have experienced deathly dull Evangelical, overly hyped Pentecostal and rigidly routine Liturgical services short on God's presence. But I have also experienced Scripture-expounded and Spirit-endowed Evangelical, Pentecostal and Liturgical services.

We can pursue God's presence intellectually through Scripture, emotionally through the Spirit and physically through the Sacraments. Ryan Flanigan explains:

> Very simply, to be charismatic means to seek the presence of the Lord through the gifts of the *Spirit*, especially in an environment of musical worship. To be evangelical means to seek the presence of the Lord through the *Scriptures*, especially in Bible study and gospel preaching. To be liturgical means to seek the presence of the Lord through the *Sacraments*, especially in the Holy Eucharist and ordered prayer.[11]

Gordon T. Smith masterfully argues for an integration of all three traditions in *Evangelical, Sacramental, & Pentecostal: Why the Church Should Be All Three*.[12] To make enthralling music, an orchestra reads the score and performs its coordinated notes together, not as isolated musicians. Legendary record producer Quincy Jones advised when making music, "You've got to leave space for God to walk through the room."[13] When God's presence super-naturalizes our gatherings, He galvanizes them more than a Coldplay or U2 concert or the epic theme song for the movie *Pirates of the Caribbean*. Have a listen!

Scripture

I value expository preaching. I have witnessed scores of preachers not preach the Scripture text itself or the message of the Gospel (*logos*). They might speak their outlines and illustrations from a launching pad verse or passage. Everything they say could be true, but not necessarily *in* the text. And they can resort to storytelling and hype. Note this impact: "While Peter was still saying these things, the Holy Spirit fell on all who heard the word [*logos*]" (Acts 10:44). Have you ever witnessed this? I have.

Church leaders must *devote* themselves to prayer and the ministry of the word (see Acts 6:4). Preachers often prepare too much, preach too long and pray too little with unremarkable results. Notice: prayer first then the Word (*logos*). The default devotion is usually to preparation and preaching but not to prayer. The fire is in the prayer closet. Note the results: "The word of God continued to increase, and the number of disciples multiplied greatly in Jerusalem" (Acts 6:7).

Have you ever heard of the older word *unction*? I love this word. It refers to the projecting power of divine impact from the Spirit's laser-focused anointing that penetrates hearer's hearts during preaching or teaching (see Acts 2:37; 10:44). Reported of revivalist Charles Finney, "When he opened his mouth, he was aiming a gun. When he spoke, the bombardment began."[14]

He did not write his sermons ahead of time. In preparation, he dove into prayer and fasting. He considered prayer as an "indispensable condition of promoting the revival."[15] Finney is not your typical pastor, but we can learn from him. To swirl in his reflections, read *The Autobiography of Charles Finney*.

E. M. Bounds affirms:

> Light praying will make light preaching. Prayer makes preaching strong, gives it *unction*, and makes it stick. . . . This unction comes to the preacher, not in the study but in the closet . . . that the sermon might be scented by the air of heaven. The little estimate we put on prayer is evident from the little time we give it.[16]

I challenged the pastors in our district to test this. Many did and reported their people would comment that something was different with their messages. Leonard Ravenhill says, "With all thy getting, get unction."[17]

George Whitefield was a bombastic preacher in the First Great Awakening. In 1735, he recorded in his diary:

> My mind being now more open and enlarged, I began to read the Holy Scriptures upon my knees, laying aside all other books and praying over, if possible, every line and word. This proved meat indeed and drink indeed to my soul. I daily received fresh life, light, and power from above.[18]

I do this, too. It is said of Baptist Charles Spurgeon that on his way up to the pulpit to preach he would repeat, "I believe in the Holy Spirit, I believe in the Holy Spirit."[19]

Except for the Liturgical tradition, public oral reading of Scripture and prepared prayers are a lost art in many churches. Paul's emphatic "Devote yourself to the public reading of Scripture" (1 Timothy 4:13), if offered, is usually done haphazardly and flatly without prior preparation or prayer. The key is to know the correct pronunciation of all the words and to rehearse the structure, grammar, flow and emotional tone in advance. Internalize the Scripture or prayers with prayer and meditation, and communicate with a projecting vocal pitch from your heart by the Spirit. You will notice the impact. Practice it with Galatians 3:1–9 and Psalm 28:1–9.

Remember, "Faith comes from *hearing*, and hearing through the word [*rhēma*] of Christ" (Romans 10:17, emphasis added). God's word is a means (instrument) of grace, as He speaks Gospel truths to feed our faith. As we hear the Word preached and read in an attitude of prayer, welcomed with an honest and good heart, it sizzles as Spirit and life to strengthen our muscles of trust in Christ. To gain skill in how to read Scripture publicly, I recommend Jeffrey D. Arthurs, *Devote Yourself to the Public Reading of Scripture.*

In corporate gatherings, let Scripture inhabit the teaching and worship. "Let the word of Christ dwell in you richly, teaching and admonishing one another in all wisdom, singing psalms and hymns and spiritual songs, with thankfulness in your hearts to God" (Colossians 3:16).

Spirit

Imagine the scenes in the Revelation to John. They depict colossal worship services that are dazzling in sights and sounds, songs and shouts, with music erupting from the harmonies of heaven in rainbow-embellished holiness and burning torches of fire that radiate the seven Spirits of God. Presence-centered worship can unleash the culture of heaven on earth. Do we view worship as either in Spirit (Pentecostal) or in truth (Evangelical)? Remember, the Father as Spirit seeks true worshipers who worship Him in both Spirit and truth, through Jesus Christ who embodies both (see John 4:23–24).

Worship today is viewed mainly as singing usually led by a worship leader or worship team. But worship is more than singing, and musicians in Scripture were never the primary worship leaders, though they contributed.[20] Priests were. Numerous contemporary songs contain human-centered lyrics and lack theology and a God focus. Please regularly include some psalms, classic hymns and the historic confessions of the faith! They have staying power.

The psalms display a God focus as prominent as the Eiffel Tower. Worship is to ascribe worth to God. Worshipers "shall not appear before the LORD empty-handed" (Deuteronomy 16:16). We enter God's presence primarily through prayer and praise to ascribe Him worth with our lips and our lives. Scripture, Spirit and sacrament curate the plush landscape of worship.

Pastors should view themselves as the chief worship architect and leader—not simply the preacher—who coordinates the entire worship service. They should incorporate prayer as the central practice around which song, sermon and sacrament revolve. Devotion to prayer and the Word are parallel priorities. Preachers will have to shorten both sermons and singing to fit carefully planned segments of Scripture-fed and Spirit-led prayer into gatherings.

Pre-service prayer or a brief pastoral prayer is not enough. A twenty-minute, well-planned prayer time is ideal. This could include intercessory prayer, prayer for healing, prophetic prayer, prayer for the government, warfare prayer, missional prayer, Scripture prayer and ordered prayer. It could be divided up into segments between songs, Scripture reading, and liturgy.

One Sunday morning after the worship set and before the message, the pastor invited those who suffered from the lingering effects of COVID-19 to come forward for healing prayer. For ten minutes, we prayed for people who had a loss of smell or taste or who had experienced irregular heartbeats, chronic fatigue, coughing, chest pain, anxiety or depression and other infirmities. About fifty people in both services came forward. A large segment testified to tangible results.

We can pray for healing during a service just as Jesus did when four friends lowered a paralytic down through the ceiling in a crowded Capernaum house. Jesus gave His message, but He stopped to heal him (see Mark 2:1–12).

Lead pastors must both lead and model prayer for it to take root in a church, though they will involve others. They cannot outsource prayer just as they cannot outsource preaching. They can place brief announcements at the beginning of the service for a seamless flow of seeking God's presence. Presence-centered churches are Spirit-controlled. They are the kind of churches when an unbeliever enters, "falling on his face, he will worship God and declare that God is really among you" (1 Corinthians 14:25). Pastor and author Jim Cymbala warns:

> The truth is in too many churches, people don't experience God's presence. The Sunday services are monotonous and predictable. Or theatrical and human-centered. Sadly, even many church leaders themselves have never experienced the awesomeness of God's presence. All they know about is how to "do church." They aren't to sit there and wing it. . . . There's something wrong when our services are so tightly programmed and streamlined there's no openness for the Holy Spirit to interrupt with his agenda.[21]

On August 28, 2022, a Bethel moment occurred. I was scheduled to preach in two Sunday services on Psalm 105:1–4. The first service went as planned. Not so for the second. During the worship, the Lord redirected the service when the pastoral host sensed we needed to pause, pray and minister to Him for twenty minutes. The pastor canceled the announcements, offering and greetings to follow and invited me up. By now, I sensed the Lord redirect me to remove my shoes and pray the passage rather than preach it. So I did, for 27 minutes. Nothing dramatic occurred, but it was deep, a shift, a hushed and holy moment of presence in the house.

When I was a Vineyard pastor, we would pray "Come, Holy Spirit." It was a brave invitation for the Spirit's presence and power to manifest among us. He did! This prayer, called *Veni Sancte Spiritus* in Latin, dates back to the 13th century. Some churches use it for Pentecost Sunday. Here are the first three stanzas:

> Come, Holy Spirit;
> send down from heaven's height
> your radiant light.
>
> Come, lamp of every heart,
> come, parent of the poor;
> all gifts are yours.
>
> Comforter beyond all comforting,
> sweet unexpected guest,
> sweetly refresh.[22]

Pray it and watch!

Sacrament

I attended an Anglican service where the liturgy of Scripture reading, ordered prayers, homily and the Eucharist from the *Book of Common Prayer* ushered in God's presence. It was so intense that I sat with a lump in my throat as my mind and heart raced into scriptural scenes as multicolored and euphoric as scenes in the movie *La La Land*. After the service, I learned from the priest all his Scripture readers were trained to read and pray.

If the early Church did it (see Acts 2:42; 20:7), why cannot all churches regularly combine Scripture, Spirit and sacrament?[23] The Eucharist is not simply an ordinance but an actual participation and partaking in remembrance of Christ's body and blood and communion with Him (see 1 Corinthians 10:16–18). It is a visible sign of an inward grace. The bread and beverage make Jesus present to us that we might abide in Him through spiritual nutrition. He prophetically anticipates the Last Supper as sacramental, and He promised, "Whoever feeds on my flesh and drinks my blood abides in me, and I in him" (John 6:56). The verbs are present tense—as we keep on feeding and drinking (by faith), we keep on abiding in Him.

Presence-centered churches are sacramental. Succulent meals offer communion and personal presence with participants. The Eucharist offers a succulence of Christ's personal presence with us through Scripture and Spirit. "Christ is a personal, engaging *presence*," Gordon Smith remarks, "who meets us and gives himself to us. But he does so specifically through this event when our celebration is informed by the *Word* of God and infused by the *Spirit* of God."[24]

Try the different accounts: Matthew 26:26–29, Luke 22:14–20 and 1 Corinthians 11:23–26. It is a challenge to hold the Eucharist online, but it is here to stay. When we seek God's presence through Sacrament, let's prepare our hearts in prayer and piety and nourish our faith as we partake in a taste of theology.

Leading a Presence-Centered Church

I attended a gathering of denominational leaders in Alberta from the Alliance, Pentecostal, Evangelical Missionary, Baptist, Evangelical Free and Church of God. That week, I also held a Zoom meeting with Nazarene church leaders in Ohio and had a cell call with an Anglican leader in Vancouver. Our interactions focused on one vision we all held: to lead and revitalize churches where pastors and people face challenges and frustrations for which we were not trained.

A Nazarene pastor labeled our worldview shift as a healthy hopelessness because the game changed right before our eyes. And now we must learn how to shift from checkers to chess on the fly. Pre-COVID navigation strategies and skills that worked on the calm seas of routine church life will not get us through the stormy whitecaps of post-COVID chaos. Purpose, program or personality-centered churches tethered to staff and volunteer-driven weekend services dominated by sermons, singing and Sunday school that are contained in a building face arduous journeys ahead.

The operating systems that ran vertical churches, seeker churches and Bible churches will bog down as if they were to run on outdated Windows 10 or Yosemite. The gnawing question church leaders face is, What is the main draw that will gather and keep people connected to Christ and the church? The enduring appeal, whether in person or on social media, is God's presence.

Leading from the Inner Room

The first principle of *Spirit*-ual leadership is we lead out of who we are as Spirit-saturated saints. Let this jar you. Jesus prayed from His *piety* and God heard Him. "In the days of His humanity, He offered up both prayers and pleas . . . and He was heard because of His devout behavior" (Hebrews 5:7 NASB). For God's presence to shape our churches, it must first shape the secret cathedral of leaders' hearts, where Christ dwells through faith (see Ephesians 3:17).

It is tough to host God's presence if we do not pursue a presence-centered life. Because, "You will always reproduce the environment around you," states Kris Vallotton, "that you cultivate within you."[25]

Private spiritual integrity releases spiritual authority in public. Many leaders focus on the outer life of the public world and sprint on a treadmill of busyness and endless meetings. The condition of their outer life reflects the condition of their inner life. Frazzled and fearful outer lives reflect frazzled and fearful inner lives. A line in *Frozen II* reminds us, "Fear is what can't be trusted."[26]

Years ago, I quit attending Global Leadership Summits as well as reading more books on leadership, though they are helpful. For me, they lacked an emphasis on God's presence, prayer and leading by the Spirit. I cannot lead through CEO-style position, personality, pulpiteering or Christianized business practices and strategic planning, but rather through Holy Spirit-inflamed impact, oxygenated with the bellows of prayer and presence-centered leadership. Saint Francis of Assisi, regarded as a "living sanctuary of the Holy Spirit," inspires me to guide others as a presence-centered leader who leads from my inner room, where the Lord dwells and guides—and makes upper room leadership possible.

Leading from the Upper Room

After Jesus departed for heaven (see Acts 1:9–11), He left a home prayer meeting behind that occurred on a flat, open-air, rooftop upper room in Jerusalem (see Acts 1:13–14). That became a ten-day, one-accord prayer meeting with a direct lifeline to heaven governed by a prophetic promise and a passage. They waited for Spirit baptism and empowerment that fulfilled Joel 2:18–22 (see Acts 1:4–8; 2:16–21). From the Upper Room, Jesus propelled His mission through prayerful, presence-centered leaders. This reminds me of Eugene Peterson's wisdom, "Waiting in prayer is a disciplined refusal to act before God acts."[27]

The book of Acts offers a model of how to lead a presence-centered church from the Upper Room. Fred Hartley comments:

167

The upper room is the closest place to heaven on earth. . . . The upper room doesn't need to be 'upper' in location, but upper in *priority* and *prominence*. Upper room, God-encountering prayer is the launching pad and lifeline of every church ministry and activity.[28]

Upper Room prayers in Acts are missional and outward, informed by Scripture and the prophetic, not inward and devotional.

Here are effective practices on how to lead from an Upper Room philosophy adapted from John Piippo's outstanding book *Leading the Presence-Driven Church*:

- Travel without a map. Presence-driven churches are Spirit-led and unpredictable.
- Be led before you lead. Surrender control and trust God's leading and abide in him.
- Discern rather than decide. Presence-driven churches don't brainstorm but discern.
- Share what you experience. Testimonies of God encounters throw logs on the fire.
- Lean toward minimalism. Worship, pray, and preach and allow room for God.
- Don't strive to make things happen. Teach people to abide in Christ.
- Find healing in his presence. A presence-driven church fosters a healing environment.
- Use different language. Words like *presence*, *abiding*, and *follower* shape church culture.
- Leaders must spend time in God's presence, where purpose comes from prayerfulness.
- Presence-driven leaders practice and teach others to abide in Christ, saturate in the Scriptures, listen (discern God's voice) and obey.[29]

The Upper Room is not so much a place to house a church's unique call and disciple-making vision as it is a priority of prevailing prayer for leaders to seek God's presence for mission and guidance. Do we pray as much as we discuss? Ruth Haley Barton asks:

> Who would we be if the practice of intercessory prayer shaped our leadership? How might it change the dynamic between us and those we are leading if they knew that we are regularly and routinely entering into God's presence with the intent to speak and lead from what transpires there.[30]

It is daunting for church leaders to consistently lead a presence-centered church from the Upper Room, as it is easy to extinguish the Spirit's fire and gravitate toward human agency and control. Some church leaders are *autocratic*. Others are *democratic*. The New Testament showcases *pneumatic* leaders open to the Spirit (*pneuma*) with His guidance and control. He manifests Himself as the Trinity coordinates its energies and works through Christians in spiritual gifts that include prophecy (see 1 Corinthians 12:4–11). Paul warns, "Do not quench the Spirit. Do not despise prophecies, but test everything; hold fast what is good" (1 Thessalonians 5:19–21).

Church leaders should equip their people in how to pray, prophesy and host God's presence in their workaday worlds. They will model and teach how to pray "at *all* times in the Spirit, with *all* prayer and supplication. To that end, keep alert with *all* perseverance, making supplication for *all* the saints" (Ephesians 6:18, emphasis added). The two participles are present tense: keep praying in the Spirit while keeping alert with all perseverance.

I know a young woman, Linda, who served agitated residents in a long-term care home for her clinical practicum as a nursing student. Her Alliance church teaches on the power of prayer, Jesus' name and God's presence. One woman with dementia would kick, bite and scream at care aids. Linda decided to whisper "peace in Jesus' name" in her ear. The woman stopped immediately. Then, whenever Linda entered her room, she quietly spoke "Jesus" into the room. The woman became peaceful and recognized her though she did not recognize her own husband. This astounded the care aids.

Linda also served a man in his mid-sixties with brain damage who spoke at the level of a four-year-old. He was perverse and abusive to care aids. As she entered his room, she whispered, "in Jesus' name" and discreetly prayed for peace and purity over him. He became kind and respectful. Then one day at the breakfast table, he sat smiling. When asked about it, he mentioned a dream he kept having. He prophesied, "A tsunami wave of faith is coming from the East. God is coming back!" He was an unbeliever who had never heard of Jesus. A stunned care aid witnessed all this, and Linda shared Jesus with her and invited her to church. She came, wept the entire time and gave her life to Jesus. Linda and her church host God's presence.

Ponder what it means to become and lead a habitation of *kāvôd*—a presence-centered church. Regularly peer into the sky and let your imagination soar, as the heavens proclaim the sprawling glory of God. When you gather as boards or teams, in annual meetings and in weekend services, remember, "Now to him who is able to do immeasurably more than all we ask or imagine, according to his power that is at work within us, to him be glory in the church and in Christ Jesus throughout all generations, for ever and ever! Amen" (Ephesians 3:20–21 NIV).

10

Home-Based Bethel

Presence-Centered Families

I am reminded of your sincere faith, a faith that dwelt
first in your grandmother Lois and your mother Eunice
and now, I am sure, dwells in you as well.

2 Timothy 1:5

My wife and I are friends of a retired couple in Kelowna in
their eighties, Jake and Mavis. They served in Alliance for-
eign missions, seminary and pastoral leadership for decades.
One morning while we visited them, they shared a remarkable
story about the fullness of the Spirit's tangible presence in their
home. They had hired two men to lay new flooring in their
condo. When the day ended and the men were ready to leave,
Jake and Mavis took some time to chat with them. After they
thanked the workers, one of the men commented on how their
home was peaceful and how something was different there.

He said, "There's no evil here."

Mavis replied, "Evil isn't allowed in our home." He noted how they were patient and never yelled at each other or at them as workers. She asked if people yelled at them.

He answered, "Yes. Always. It's terrible."

She went on, "This is a place of peace, love and joy. And it's a house of prayer." When they finished this story, I sat dumbfounded on the couch, wiping my eyes. God's presence inhabited that living room—with home-based *kāvôd*. A few days later, Mavis texted me.

"Roger, what I desire most is to be so full of the Spirit's presence and His sweet love and fragrance that I don't have to do anything but be!" This dear couple hosted God's presence at home. Sadly, Mavis graduated to glory on April 8, 2022, at age 84.

Home-Based Bethel

This was a home-based Bethel that housed God. The Hebrew word *Bethel* means "house of God."[1] It is a holy habitation where God dwells. Remember how God appeared to Jacob in a dream with a ladder that reached heaven (see Genesis 28:12–13)? It is a localized place of God's manifest presence. How would you describe your home? How was it as a child?

Hallmark cards and Thomas Kincaid paintings depict home as an enchanted place of beauty and belonging. In the movie *Wizard of Oz*, Dorothy concludes, "There's no place like home."[2] For some, home was warm and secure. For others, it was cold and insecure. For some, recollections of home and father can trigger thoughts of abandonment, abuse, anger or alcoholism. Don't we all yearn for love, security and acceptance? Bethel is an extravagant mansion occupied by God, who is love. Jesus invites, "Make your home in me just as I do in you" (John 15:4 MSG).

I grew up in Southern California squalor as a pagan. My mother married and divorced three times. Her second husband was my birth father, who I never knew. Her third husband became my stepdad. Divorce rampaged our family and hammered its toll on us. I felt fatherless and rootless, my stepdad was rarely present with me and we moved every few years. My mother loved me with a tender heart. They offered their best, and both worked hard. But they both grew up in wounded families, too, and we lived secular lives without Jesus. The generational sins of alcoholism, control, perfectionism and unfaithfulness lurk in the background passed down in my family system from the third and fourth generations (see Exodus 34:6–7).

When I got married at age 27 to Gail, a Canadian farm girl I met at Bible college, I knew nothing of a home-based Bethel. Many times since, I have renounced and continue to repent of my family and personal sins, destructive beliefs and lies. I continually seek God's presence and healing of emotional and spiritual pain. After 43 years of Christian marriage, with three children and six grandchildren in the quiver, I am convinced marriages and families will crash on rocky shores if they do not learn to build homes that host God's presence.

Homes That Host God's Presence

I recall valuable advice a pastor we knew offered to us about couples with young children: "Don't let the children become the center of your family life. Let Christ be the center."

Easy to say but tough to do—like wrestling with an open umbrella as the wind gusts. Couples with young children (and teens) can barely manage the mayhem and velocity of those kids. Weary parents strain to get them out the door and back to the dinner table, into the bathroom and off to bed, as they administrate the merry-go-round of homework, friends, music lessons, sports, birthday parties, sibling rivalries, chores, church and interruptions, matched with endless needs for hugs, talks and godly discipline of these miniature sinners! Where is Jesus in it all?

Jesus stated, "Make your home in Me as I make mine in you." Jesus is a homebody in the home of our hearts. And our hearts govern our homes. It is a spiritual strategy to place Christ and not the children at the center. What grips parents grips kids— parent power. Does it alarm you when your children or grandchildren imitate you and repeat your words or actions? Scary!

Our homes flourish when we make them houses of prayer that host God's presence. I have read stacks of books on marriage and parenting with benefit, but Jesus is the expert. There were times as parents when we ran out of gas and slammed into brick walls. I recall one evening when Gail and I sat on our couch after a stressful season with our teens and mused about how we ever got there. We felt like dead batteries and dry wells. That occurred when we failed to pray together and allowed our packed lives to crowd Jesus out.

I owned my responsibility to love my wife as Christ loved the church and not be harsh with her (see Ephesians 5:25; Colossians 3:19). This is not erotic or romantic love, but self-sacrificial and self-giving agape love—the kind Christ expresses for His Church. It means the husband as head of his wife is the head lover, not the head dominator. Wives are willing to submit or rank themselves under loving husbands, as to the Lord, and as the Church ranks under Christ (see Ephesians 5:22–24). Husbands can be harsh at times. A macho man is not presence centered. A godly man is. Women and men enjoy equal spiritual status in a Christ-centered home.

I tried not to exasperate my children but bring them up in the Lord's discipline and instruction (see Ephesians 6:4). My stepdad grew up on a farm in Catawba, Wisconsin, with a strict father and used the same style on me. John Newton remarked,

"I am persuaded [my father] loved me, but he seemed not willing that I should know it. . . . His sternness, together with the severity of my schoolmaster, broke and overawed my spirit."[3]

We can overdo discipline and cruelly nitpick misbehaviors in our children. But routine pats on the back go further than constant kicks in the rear. It is easy to drive sensitive children to discouragement and performance and breed cavernous insecurity, anxiety and depression. Teen suicide is rampant. Presence-centered fathers and mothers must love as Christ loves and douse buckets of affirmation on their kids, even though they can push our buttons.

We never delegated spiritual instruction to Sunday school or youth programs. It came from us firsthand through daily interactions, teachable moments and family meetings. Disciple-making of children begins at home.

Hear, O Israel: The LORD our God, the LORD is one. You shall love the LORD your God with all your heart and with all your soul and with all your might. And these words that I command you today shall be on your heart. You shall teach them diligently to your children, and shall talk of them when you sit in your house, and when you walk by the way, and when you lie down, and when you rise.

Deuteronomy 6:4–7

Gail and I acquired an assortment of picture Bible books and stories we read, and we gave them children's Bibles when they were young and study Bibles when they were older.

Jesus expects us to make our children His disciples who we baptize and teach to obey His commands. Some traditions use confirmation and catechism programs, which are valuable, but parents are the home-based disciple-makers. Paul commands, "Children, obey your parents in the Lord, for this is right. 'Honor your father and mother'" (Ephesians 6:1–2). Parents love this verse! And this one, "Children, obey your parents in everything, for this pleases the Lord" (Colossians 3:20). Love, affirmation and consistency, mingled with gentle but firm words, make it easier for children to obey. Parents carry God-given spiritual authority but need not wield it with force.

I discovered we could not force, correct or lecture godly values, attitudes and conduct into our children. Unconditional love, through example and godly discipline, is the top way to shape their character, centered in prayer and God's presence. Pray God would release the fruit of the Spirit in their lives. That He would guide, protect and speak to them. Pray they would hear God's voice, love and obey His Word and respond to His Spirit.

Let's teach our children how to hear from God. "At that time Jesus declared, 'I thank you, Father, Lord of heaven and earth, that you have hidden these things from the wise and understanding and revealed them to little children; yes, Father, for such was your gracious will'" (Matthew 11:25–26). Bradley Jersak, in his book *Can You Hear Me?* offers practices to help parents teach their children to hear God:

1. Assume your child already hears God.
2. Invite your child to find Jesus in a meeting place.
3. Convert bedtime prayers into listening prayers.
4. Invite Jesus into nightmares and night terrors.
5. Take conflicts at school and home to Jesus.
6. Help your children interpret their dreams.
7. Incorporate listening prayer into Sunday school.[4]

Pray for their rites of passage, dreams and decisions, fears, schoolwork and friendships. Pray at mealtimes and bedtimes. Pray for them as they go out the door to catch the bus for school or before your homeschooling day. Quietly pray before you offer discipline, look them square in the eyes, hug and tell them you love them. Pray when they are sick. When our daughter Melissa was seven, she contracted eczema on her hands. We prayed for her, and God healed it.

From 2015 till 2020, we also prayed for our son Joel, who was diagnosed with relapse and remission multiple sclerosis. He underwent a four-year process of two treatments with a powerful drug and monthly blood tests, and his recovery was monitored by an MS specialist at the University of British Columbia, Vancouver. We believe in medicine and miracle. While he studied occupational therapy at UBC, we organized a Zoom prayer gathering with his wife's family in Mexico. After his wife anointed him with oil, we all prayed and continued to pray for four years. Today, his MRI tests show no signs of MS except some small scar tissue.

Pray when you face family barriers. As we prayed, God brought the concept of peer attachment to our attention. We learned God designed children to attach to their parents and significant others as their primary reference point—where they absorb their values, connection and responses. But when children bond to their peers to get their values and sense of belonging, they dodge an attachment to their parents. They unconsciously perceive their parents as those who intervene, as adversaries and those who threaten their peer bubble. With access to 24/7 social media, the gravitational pull of peer attachment is intense. We worked to be present with our kids and stay connected to them. Regina Brett comments, "Your children get only one childhood. Make it memorable. Make sure you're there for it."[5]

A human soul is like a rose, delicate and easily injured, especially by those in authority. As I noticed times when my wife or my children became like deflated balloons, I had to approach them with tears to talk, eat crow, confess my sin, ask for forgiveness, hug and seek restoration. They always forgave. I sought and continue to seek the Lord through Scripture and prayer in how I can be the husband, dad and Papa these extraordinary people need through my attention and my words that carry weight. Karl Menninger said, "What's done to children, they will do to society." The book of Proverbs, Ephesians 5 and Colossians 3 are reliable guides for presence-centered families.

Home-Based Holiness

Homes that gleam with God's holiness host God's presence. How? Not through a catalog of rigid rules pinned to the refrigerator door or through endless correction. It happens when we settle the question that I posed in chapter 1: What is your center? Our center cannot be the children, the parents, the rules, the activities or the Church. Peter urges, "But in your hearts honor [consecrate] Christ the Lord as holy" (1 Peter 3:15), and Paul explains, "All things were created through him and for him. . . . that in everything he might be preeminent" (Colossians 1:16, 18). If Jesus is the universe's center, His rightful place in our hearts and homes is the center.

Let's return to Hebrews 12:14 for home-based holiness. "Pursue peace with all people, and holiness, without which no one will see the Lord" (NKJV). What is your family culture like? Most families are busy and bustling with energy. The TV is on, the pot is boiling over, Mom is talking to her sister on her cell, the kids compete for the iPad, the doorbell rings, the dog wants in and dad is mowing the lawn. Dinner times can become pit stops in the race of competing food preferences, running late for Girl Guides and a senior sibling bugging a junior one. Weekends buzz with friends and fixing the toilet, shopping and doing the laundry mixed with chores and church. But in the chaos, is there peace? Or is there tension and tempers?

A home-based Bethel will house holiness in the hearts of mom and dad that cultivates an atmosphere of peace. Lack of harmony suggests a lack of holiness. When Christ occupies the center as the Prince of Peace, as a Rocky Mountain log cabin warmed from a crackling fireplace, He warms the inner and outer life of parents as they pursue peace and holiness at home.

Marriages and families (and churches) that duke it out with harsh words, bitterness or anger grieve the Spirit and block God's manifest presence like an NFL lineman. Notice the context of Ephesians 4:29–32:

> Let no corrupting talk come out of your mouths, but only such as is good for building up, as fits the occasion, that it may give grace to those who hear. And do not grieve the Holy Spirit of God, by whom you were sealed for the day of redemption. Let all bitterness and wrath and anger and clamor and slander be put away from you, along with all malice. Be kind to one another, tenderhearted, forgiving one another, as God in Christ forgave you.

As parents, our words carry weight with each other and our children. May those words be wholesome, respectful and Spirit-led. I have learned in life and leadership that "Death and life are in the power of the tongue, and those who love it will eat its fruits" (Proverbs 18:21).

The battles we might have with each other or with the kids are battles within our own hearts. James asks, "What causes quarrels and what causes fights among you? Is it not this, that your passions are at war within you?" (James 4:1). If we desire changes in our spouse or children, the changes must occur within us first. It is amazing what happens when I soften my tone, choose my words carefully and offer patience, affirmation and encouragement.

Every marriage and family faces hostile opponents of holiness in the culture through certain movies, music, TV, the internet, schools and universities, advertising and ultimately from Satan and indwelling sin. We cannot hide from the world, the flesh and the devil, but instead must face them in Christ. We cannot legislate holiness into our marriage and family. As a husband and father, I vowed to keep my mind and heart pure for my wife alone, not defile the marriage bed, and monitor what I looked at, listened to and thought about.

I copied Job and "made a covenant with my eyes not to look lustfully at a young woman. For what is our lot from God above, our heritage from the Almighty on high? . . . Does he not see my ways and count my every step?" (Job 31:1–2, 4 NIV). May this be a warning and motivation for us all: "Let marriage be held in honor among all, and let the marriage bed be undefiled, for God will judge the sexually immoral and adulterous" (Hebrews 13:4). My exposure to illicit sexuality when I was young makes me vulnerable. I guard my heart and emotions when I see or am in the company of attractive women. I decided to avoid certain television programs, such as *Dancing with the Stars*, sensual movies and certain rock and country music that can inflame my carnal appetites.

To pursue holiness means we are not distracted and passive but intentional and active as traffic cops who regulate what races into the intersection of our homes. Parents face enormous challenges and influences today with their children who have access to the internet, cable TV, iPads, video games, apps and relentless peer pressure. These are never good substitute babysitters or disciplers. Set boundaries. We battled with our children over movies and music.

Our policy was not to permit R-rated and most PG-13 movies or heavy metal music. When we would try to select films, our kids naturally gravitated toward the most popular ones that rarely matched our policy. We would point out that the vulgar language, steamy scenes or violence was not acceptable and contaminated their imaginations. They would reply this is how real life is out there and it did not matter because there was only a minor amount in the movie. I would reply, "If someone offered you a freshly

180

baked chocolate brownie with a tiny amount of poop in it would you eat it?" I said a tiny amount contaminates the whole brownie. Feeling cornered, they did not appreciate that graphic illustration!

But holiness in the home is less about movie and music policies and more about placing Christ at the center, which influences the family culture with God's presence. I remember one evening when we had a couple from our church over for dinner. We enjoyed a fine meal and conversation followed by a customary prayer we offered our guests. As they got up to leave, the husband remarked, "This home feels like a place of peace." May we pursue peace and holiness as a daily practice of presence-centered piety, with prayer and repentance in the fear of God.

Home-Based Fear of God

If you were to advise a young couple on how they can encounter God's presence and flourish in their marriage and family as a home-based Bethel, what would you say? I would point them to Psalm 128 and summarize it in two words: fear God. As an ascent psalm, where pilgrims and families traveled up to Jerusalem for an annual worship festival, "The quiet blessings of an ordered life are traced from the center outwards in this psalm, as the eye travels from the godly man to his family and finally to Israel. Here is simple piety with its proper fruit of stability and peace."[6]

> A Song of Ascents. Blessed is everyone who fears the Lord, who walks in his ways! You shall eat the fruit of the labor of your hands; you shall be blessed, and it shall be well with you. Your wife will be like a fruitful vine within your house; your children will be like olive shoots around your table. Behold, thus shall the man be blessed who fears the Lord. The Lord bless you from Zion! May you see the prosperity of Jerusalem all the days of your life! May you see your children's children! Peace be upon Israel!
>
> Psalm 128

The way to flourish in marriage and family is to fear God and walk in His ways. The evidence of deep reverence for God will issue in conformity to His will. Those who fear the Lord enjoy blessing, prosperity and well-being in their work and personal lives. When I sing the refrain from the hymn, "It Is Well with My Soul,"[7] a hefty lump swells in my throat as I choke back the tears. I reflect on God's grace and goodness through the seasons of life.

The man who fears the Lord enjoys the finery of a wife and children pictured as fruitful grapevines and olive shoots. In the ancient world, these symbolized the fruitfulness and vitality of God's blessing (see Deuteronomy 8:8; Jeremiah 31:5). Psalm 128 depicts those special occasions such as Thanksgiving and Christmas, when we gather as a family with our children and grandchildren for a lively dinner around the table. The savor of a baked turkey or ham and mashed potatoes and gravy, accompanied by beaming faces and conversation, joy and laughter signal God's favor.

For those men who fear Him, God blesses their families. May the Lord bless you from Zion—the place of His presence. May you see the Church, the heavenly Jerusalem and the Israel of God prosper and know peace, wealth and well-being. And may you see your grandchildren thrive, considered a chief blessing in the ancient world (see Job 42:16–17).

Home-Based Blessing

I recall what the late John Wimber, leader of Vineyard International, said to me about the practice of blessing. "Be careful what you bless. Whatever you bless, you empower."

He referenced spiritual leaders who must exercise discernment in who or what they bless and not offer it as a willy-nilly gesture of goodwill. If it is off-kilter, I hesitate to bless and thereby empower something or someone simply out of goodwill or what is politically correct. I exercise that policy in both ministry leadership and marriage and family. I will not bless divisive or toxic actions Christian leaders might display to simply relieve the tension, keep the peace or demonstrate so-called grace. And there are actions, attitudes and decisions my children or grandchildren might show I will not bless, particularly if they contradict Scripture or the Spirit. But, on another level, a home-based Bethel practices home-based blessing.

My passion for blessing my children and now grandchildren got more burn when I read *The Blessing* by Gary Smalley and John Trent.[8] To bless is to bestow prosperity, goodness and favor and to speak well of someone. To bless is to transmit an impartation of God's favor into someone's life by verbal pronouncement and at times with the laying on of hands. It does not matter how old they are; children starve for their parents' blessing. Countless adults spend their entire lives without their parents' approval and affirmation. Their wounded spirits can compel them to perform, overwork and become angry and depressed. Without a blessing environment of love and acceptance, many youth try to anesthetize their pain through alcohol, drugs, sex, social media and violent behavior. They can withdraw into a sullen silence or contemplate suicide.

Blessing dates back to Old Testament times. Isaac blessed Jacob (see Genesis 27), Jacob blessed his sons and grandsons (see Genesis 48:8—49:33), Melchizedek blessed Abram (see Genesis 14:18–20), and Aaron blessed the Israelites (see Numbers 6:23–27). When parents and grandparents bless their children and grandchildren, their blessing infuses security and strength into them. Our spoken words can *en*courage—put courage in—especially when accompanied by physical touch. Say yes more often to your kids.

The essence of bless is *yes*! Smalley and Trent offer five ways to bless:

1. *Meaningful Touch.* Children and grandchildren need hugs, kisses, and physical touch to fill their emotional

tanks. Like a sponge, they absorb affection. They must feel blessing. Touch them often. Jesus touched and blessed children (see Matthew 19:13–15). As infants, Gail would cuddle them as she nursed and afterward used a bottle and sang to them. She believed singing to them touched their souls and soothed them.

2. *A Spoken Message*. Paul wrote, "For you know that we dealt with each of you as a father deals with his own children, encouraging, comforting and urging you to live lives worthy of God" (1 Thessalonians 2:11–12 NIV). I freely encourage and comfort my children and grand-children. I mine for the good they do—the gold, not the dirt. I would tell them and put notes in their lunch that said "I love you." I send text messages. Every night, for ten years, we would place a hand on their chests and pray Numbers 6:24–26 for each child at bedtime, "The LORD bless you and keep you; the LORD make his face to shine upon you and be gracious to you; the LORD lift up his countenance upon you and give you peace." The children would calm down and slip into a deep sleep. We would lie there basking in God's manifest presence.

3. *Attaching High Value to the One Being Blessed*. We honor our children and grandchildren as people with distinct personalities, likes and dislikes. If we impose our will, they withdraw. When we attach high value and let them be who they are, they flourish. Domination is destructive. If they detest broccoli, why make them eat it? If they are shy in crowds, why force them to partici-pate? We held special nights where each child picked the supper meal followed by an activity or outing. After the supper, we would honor that child by sharing one attri-bute we each enjoyed about that person.

4. *Picturing a Special Future for the One Being Blessed*. I envisioned each child serving the Lord as a Christian

leader and saw through them and beyond. I pictured them as leaders who would influence others for God. I prayed for God's guidance to discern what to restrain or release in them according to how God made them with their passion. One day, Gail and I went on a bike ride with three of our grandchildren, their dad and the other set of grandparents. Five-year-old Brynley, a budding leader, said to me, "Follow me, Papa!"

5. *An Active Commitment to Fulfill the Blessing.* As a toddler, our oldest son, Joel, would drum on his car seat while we drove. Later, we set up ice cream pails for him to drum on with pencils. Eventually, we bought a used drum set and enrolled him in drum lessons. Our daughter Melissa developed a passion for piano. We kept her in piano lessons, bought her an electric piano and helped her achieve a grade-eight level at age fourteen. Her three daughters are now aspiring pianists. Melissa and Joel offer their skills on church worship teams. Our youngest son, Micah, showed an aptitude for the mechanical. We let him take items apart and help with activities that required the use of tools. He is now a self-employed mechanical engineer. We blessed them all to discover their destinies.

As I write, it is a mid-June morning. I gaze out my opened home office window and savor the blue sky and breeze. I am blessed. I pray for homes to host God's presence, and to radiate His *kāvôd* as brilliant places of holiness, the fear of God and blessing. Christ-centered. Bethel-based.

11

God @ Work

Presence-Centered Workplaces

God living inside us can be a scary thought. If we allowed
that truth to influence our lives and actions, it would
change everything. Right? God is a little more manageable
if we keep him in a building that we visit once a week.

Neil Cole[1]

Did you know it was a young Christian at the turn of the
twentieth century who created a dark stout beer called Guinness? That young Irishman despaired over alcoholism in his
country as hard liquor was the beverage of choice in his day.
He prayed to God for a solution. An answer ambled into his
mind, "Make a drink that men will drink that will be good for
them."

Arthur Guinness crafted a beer so full of minerals and natural trace elements that pregnant women could benefit from its

high iron content. It was difficult to get drunk on because it was heavy and contained less alcohol back then. Guinness beer became the national drink in Ireland, and Arthur was promoted to the House of Lords because of his philanthropy and wealth. He used his success to fund an orphanage in Ireland and change the judicial system in Great Britain.[2]

Those who pursue God's presence will do so as much in the workplace as in the worship place, as sacred space occupies all of life. Our vocation is our calling in life. We must listen to that call—the voice of vocation[3]—and how God places us in the world to make a difference by His presence. Early on, most people agonize over the question of what will be their life work. We must discern God's purpose for our lives and how He designed us to love Him and others with our passion, personality and gifts. What we do flows from who we are. There is no better summary of my point than this one made by the oft-quoted Frederick Buechner: "The place God calls you to is the place where your deep gladness and the world's great hunger meet."[4] Where is your deep gladness? Where is the world's great hunger, and how can you meet it?

God @ Work in the Workplace

As Genesis 1 and 2 show, work originated with God. The universe is His colossal workplace. His home office is in heaven. He assigned work to the human race with Adam and Eve in the Garden of Eden (see Genesis 2:15). Made in God's image, we fulfill His mandate to fill and subdue the earth as His co-creators and co-workers (see Genesis 1:28; 1 Corinthians 3:9). God continues to work as He cares for creation and carries out His mission in salvation. Jesus said, "My food is to do the will of him who sent me and to accomplish his work" (John 4:34), and "we must work the works of him who sent me while it is day; night is coming when no one can work" (John 9:4).

We spend significant time in the workplace; however, the view of countless Christians is to worship God at church on Sunday but enter the "real world" at work on Monday. Many key biblical characters knew God's presence at work in their secular vocations. Moses was a shepherd, Joseph a prime minister, Amos a fig farmer, Nehemiah a wine taster, Peter, Andrew and James fishermen, Luke a doctor, Paul a tentmaker, Lydia a merchant, and Philemon, a businessman. Jesus, the carpenter, met people on site in the marketplace and called them to follow him. Os Hillman states:

> Of His 132 public appearances in the New Testament, all but 10 of them were in the marketplace, and 45 of His 52 parables had a workplace context. . . . Of the 40 divine encounters and miracles listed in the book of Acts, 39 occurred in the workplace.[5]

God is at work in your workplace.

The Workplace and God's Presence

All work is sacred, and the workplace is holy ground on which to practice God's presence. The spiritual classic *The Practice of the Presence of God* offers brilliant insights from Brother Lawrence, a French Carmelite layman cook in a monastery kitchen near Paris. He learned to perceive menial tasks, such as peeling potatoes or washing dishes, as elements of worship and prayer with attentiveness to God's presence during those tasks.

As I write, I am in Ladysmith on Vancouver Island. I am seated at a picnic table with my laptop in a scenic park where I face a gleaming bay. The park hums with families gathered for morning summer fun. I observe different folks at work: city groundskeepers, kayak rental workers, fish and chips and ice cream vendors. Anchored out in the bay is a hefty cargo ship. All workplaces for these people.

188

I mused, *How is God present to them, or is He? Do they view their workplaces as those of mundane necessity where they simply earn money and can't wait for their shift to end? Do they absorb the glistening beauty from the Pacific Ocean and the handsome willow and cedar trees that line the shore? Are the park, the rental hut, the food truck and the ship a sanctuary of God for them, holy grounds of worship and prayer for them? Do they bless the people around them and delight in their gift of work as a sacred way to spend their day?*

I have had many jobs: busboy, dishwasher, yard worker, construction laborer, bicycle factory welder, soldier, custodian, framer, security night watchman, group home sponsor, pastor, professor and denominational leader. I loathed some of those temporary jobs that pounded my body and soul. I wonder how they might have been different had I learned to practice God's presence in them. It made a positive difference when I discovered my calling as a pastor-teacher and enjoyed God's pleasure. But Jesus encountered me in some of these jobs in ways I never expected—the way He encountered Matthew the tax collector at work (see Matthew 9:9–13).

Wherever you are, God is already there. Your ordinary workplace can become a sanctuary of His holy presence. You might work in an office, a hospital, a truck, a cubicle, in front of a computer screen or in front of students in a classroom. Restaurants, post offices, warehouses, construction sites, malls and homes are workplaces for many. I encouraged a website advertising business owner in Calgary to invite Jesus as his silent business partner to consult for wisdom and guidance. He had never thought of that. The idea intrigued him as he sat stunned. Invite Jesus into your workplace to give you advice, effectiveness and fulfillment. Every day, dedicate your workplace as a sanctuary—a place of worship and prayer—for presence.

Presence-Centered Workplace Practices

Enter your workplace with a spiritual tone as you pursue presence-centered work. Denise Daniels and Shannon Vandewarker in *Working in the Presence of God* write:

> How we enter our work sets the tone for our awareness of God's presence throughout the workday week. By paying attention to the way we begin work, we begin the habit of paying attention to where God might be at work throughout the day.[6]

Let me suggest four practices that will set the tone for you to develop attentiveness to God's presence at work.

Gyroscope Calibration

A few years ago, I had a conversation with my son Joel and his friend Josh about the centrality of Christ and His importance. Because Colossians 1:15–20 affirms Christ occupies the center of the universe, He must occupy that in our lives. We discussed how we must place Christ in the center of our moral choices, in our marriages and parenting, but also in our workplaces. I offered the image of a gyroscope to illustrate the point.

A gyroscope is a device that contains a wheel that spins rapidly in the center, mounted on an axis that detects any deviation of an object from its desired orientation. When the mount tilts, it does not affect the axis. The center of gravity keeps it upright when it spins. Airplanes, ships, torpedoes, missiles and satellites use gyroscopes. The Hubble telescope uses three gyroscopes to keep it oriented to the sun.

I suggested we must orient our workdays around Christ, who is the center of gravity. We can calibrate our attentiveness to revolve around Him without deviation. I do this daily in my prayer and Scripture reading before I enter my day. For Christmas a few years ago, they gave me a small gyroscope I placed on my desk to remind me of this spiritual practice that sets the tone for my workday. Let me suggest before you start your workday, practice gyroscope calibration. Each morning, "in your hearts honor Christ the Lord as holy" (1 Peter 3:15).

Ora et Labora

Another way to set the tone for pursuing God's presence in the workplace is the Benedictine practice of *ora et labora*— the Latin words for pray and labor (work). This rhythm of spiritual life can enlarge your capacity to be attuned to God's presence through a partnership of prayer and work. Before you start work, offer a prayer to the Lord. As you walk the hallway or approach your worksite or office, or before you enter a meeting or engage in a task, pray and bless your workplace. Before you check emails or texts, listen to voicemails or read any documents, focus on Jesus and pray to Him. Practice *Statio* throughout your day.

I encouraged Joel and Josh to practice *ora et labora* in their workplaces. I said, "Before you enter a meeting or have conversations with people at work, practice unceasing prayer and listen in stereo to the person and the Spirit. When you encounter a tense or complex situation, don't react but respond with inner prayerfulness, attentive to God's presence in the moment."

A few weeks later, I checked in with Josh, who was supervising tough truckers who haul cargo for CN Rail. He replied how this practice made a tangible difference in his workplace. He noticed frustrated men respond to him in remarkable ways as he saw God's presence soften their tones while He also gave him ideas and solutions to complex problems that would march into his mind.

You can practice *ora et labora* during coffee and lunch breaks. You can shut off your computer and cell phone, go for short walks, or stand up and walk around. Inhale some fresh air and pray as you also inhale God's Spirit. Talk to Him about your workday. Exhale your anxiety and stress. Ask Him for what you need to face the next work task.

Liturgy of Commute

Denise Daniels and Shannon Vandewarker offer a practice they call the liturgy of commute. A liturgy is a pattern or routine of worship we follow. We all have habits we follow, including how we get to work and what happens *in* us en route. You might ride a bus or a commuter train, drive a car, ride a bike, walk or mosey into your home office. You could travel the same way and at the same time or vary your routes and schedule. They write:

> What happens *in* you while you are getting to work can prepare you for the ways in which you are attentive to God the rest of the day. . . . Your commute can become a kind of liturgy and a time when God's perspective and purposes stir your heart.[7]

As a district minister, I would drive for hours across Alberta to visit churches and meet with my pastors and church leaders. I dreaded the long drives and how they would weary and bore me at times. But I changed my approach—my liturgy of commute—when I relished them as alone times to pray or listen to worship music, podcasts and Scripture. I prayed without ceasing as I thought about the challenges and opportunities the different churches and pastors faced. The Lord gave me ideas and inspiration I would share, and I would witness bright responses.

I would observe the snow-covered prairie fields in the winter and the golden-hued ones in the fall. I would view stunning sunsets, spectacular morning dawns and gloomy midday storm fronts. These theatrical displays of nature deepened my devotion to God for the splendor of His majesty and would overflow through my spiritual leadership into those meetings.

I occasionally knew God's presence in those rental cars. At times my eyes would well up with tears as I prayed and worshiped. But I also had frustrations with road construction delays, accidents and bumper-to-bumper traffic. These reminded me I could not control the situations but could give thanks to God in all circumstances as opportunities to learn patience and prayer.

If you walk or bicycle to work, you might do as my son Joel did when he walked or biked the three-mile journey to the hospital where he worked as an occupational therapist in Prince George, BC. He would pray or put in his earbuds and listen to worship, sermons or podcasts to set the tone for his workday. He used the return trip to reflect on his day and renew himself as he prepared for his arrival back home to reconnect with his wife and two kids.

Scripture Reading at Work

It is easy to get drawn into the drama and burdens of work and abandon a Christian mind and heart. Secular work is only secular if our Christian faith and God are not in it. Scores of people are disillusioned with Christian employers or employees who lack integrity in their work ethic. The best Christian doctors and police officers, city administrators and engineers, are those who let Scripture shape their character and work.

The marketplace desperately hungers for small business owners, attorneys, realtors, salespeople, mechanics and builders who radiate godly character and integrity, and whose word and intentions outshine small print technicalities or shady multi-level schemes. Scripture-shaped believers are oaks of righteousness who foster presence-centered workplaces. They bring the mind of Christ to the marketplace, not secular bottom line business practices or human methods with pressure tactics and dishonest advertising.

Most of us can usually schedule times to read or listen to Scripture in appropriate ways at work. We could read and pray a passage of Scripture before we start our shift. We could also read or listen to a short passage during lunch breaks. Some people use Scripture verses as screen savers on their computer monitors or their calendars. For those who have more uninterrupted quiet times, such as receptionists, hotel clerks or night security officers, you might have moments to read Scripture. You might place Scripture on the dashboard or listen from your smartphone through Bluetooth if your work is in a vehicle. If you are on your feet at work, you might carry around some index cards with Scripture on them to read. If you want a theological and practical education on fostering a presence-centered workplace, read the book of Proverbs.

Faith and Mission in the Workplace

American workers, on average, spend about 40 percent of their waking hours per week at work. Christians will spend about 5 percent of their waking hours in church, and 95 percent of their time in the world. The workplace is the primary location where we live out our Christian faith. How can ordinary Christians connect their faith with their workplace and view themselves on a mission through their vocations?

How can we foster the idea that Christian business leaders, bankers, carpenters, schoolteachers and waitresses have a ministry in their workplaces? Who can best reach police, dentists, computer techies and supermarket cashiers? Paul mentions numerous lay leaders with significant ministry in the church and community (see Romans 16, Colossians 4). Os Hillman comments:

> We have wrongly equated "ministry" to what takes place inside the four walls of the local church. We have failed to affirm the worker at IBM, the clerk at Wal-Mart, the nurse at the hospital, or the sixth-grade teacher at the elementary school. . . .

Surveys reveal more than 90% of church members do not feel the Church is equipping them to apply their biblical faith in their daily work life.[8]

I know a former high school teacher who viewed his students and classroom as his youth ministry. He modeled and taught biblical values to those teens as he loved, encouraged and accepted them. You can bet they were sponges. A friend of mine is a retired stockbroker who saw his vocation as a sacred way to help people invest and increase their wealth. He would pray for God's wisdom in stock picks and also offer discounts on his commissions where it helped those with thinner resources. Spiritual ministry is not reserved for vocational pastors and missionaries but extends to all God's people who serve as His royal priesthood in the community.

You may want to memorize this pungent text to inspire your vision for a presence-centered workplace: "When the righteous prosper, the city rejoices" (Proverbs 11:10 NIV). Righteous, Godward people scattered throughout their cities in their workplaces serve as spiritual seasoning when they prosper or succeed. They live with integrity and holiness and refuse to lie, cheat, steal or commit sexual sin or abuse in their workplaces. They treat their co-workers, customers or clients with respect. The engineer will refuse to cut corners to save the firm money. The accountant will not inflate the numbers to pad the bottom line. The secretary will not approach her boss for comfort when her marriage is strained. The city councilor will avoid conflicts of interest and not influence legislation for personal gain or private supporters.

And a missional spirituality enjoys a home-field advantage where you have natural bridges to share and reach your co-workers with the Gospel. Nurses reach other nurses, musicians reach other musicians, those in law enforcement reach others in law enforcement and so on. All vocations are sacred and sacramental when you serve according to your call from God. If He calls you to the fields of medicine, education or technology, do not sell the farm to grab a call in the field of pastoring, Bible translation or worship. Some are called to fields in the church, while the majority are called to fields in the community.

You do not have to go and do missions and ministry. You are already there in your workplace where God is at work (see John 5:17–19). When I pastored at Vernon Alliance Church, we held a formal commissioning time in several Sunday services. We identified and listed dozens of different vocations and occupations, had people stand as we called those out, and affirmed, prayed for and blessed everyone in their faith and workplaces, including stay-at-home parents. Check out the Faith and Work initiative that engages issues at the intersection of our Christian faith and its implications for our work.[9] Here is a missional spirituality for work:

> Devote yourselves to prayer, being watchful and thankful. And pray for us, too, that God may open a door for our message, so that we may proclaim the mystery of Christ, for which I am in chains. Pray that I may proclaim it clearly, as I should. Be wise in the way you act toward outsiders; make the most of every opportunity. Let your conversation be always full of grace, seasoned with salt, so that you may know how to answer everyone.
>
> Colossians 4:2–6 NIV

What are the possibilities if you prayed and practiced Colossians 4:2–6 before you left for work and while at work? What could happen if you devoted yourself to prayer, being watchful and thankful to God at work for the doors of opportunity He opens for you to share your faith with co-workers who might ask about the hope that lies within you? How might your workplace change as you live wisely and engage in seasoned conversations with people? Do you see yourself as salt and light, a living temple of God, a royal priest, as a blessing to your co-workers and customers?

You might buy a box of donuts and a plate of fruit for coffee breaks. You might leave a birthday card with a twenty-dollar Starbucks gift card inside for a co-worker. You might offer to help them when they move or when they need a ride to the airport. If a co-worker is going through a divorce, you might invite them to a divorce care DVD discussion group at your church or in a home. Perhaps your church offers a thrilling daily vacation Bible school or a dynamic youth group, or you attend a friendly small group or missional community. Invite them and their kids.

You embody the tangible Kingdom for people to witness God's presence through your holy deeds. Your missional spirituality becomes sacramental, where godly action confers God's grace and reveals His glory. "In the same way, let your light shine before others, so that they may see your good works and give glory to your Father who is in heaven" (Matthew 5:16). And "keep your conduct among the Gentiles honorable, so that when they speak against you as evildoers, they may see your good deeds and glorify God on the day of visitation" (1 Peter 2:12).

It is incredible what a simple thank-you card with a plate of muffins will do to bless a fellow schoolteacher. You might be surprised at what patiently listening to and praying for a co-worker who has recently lost a loved one to cancer will do. As a salt and light missionary, you penetrate your world and bring God into the non-religious spheres where most people live at work. The result is that "the persons acted upon and the person acting, find God in a new way."[10] David Hansen remarks, "People meet Jesus in our lives because when we follow Jesus, we are parables of Jesus Christ to the people we meet."[11]

The older I get, the more reflective I am about the speed and brevity of life. The walls are closing in. A wake-up call occurred on February 24, 2022—the same day Russia invaded

Ukraine—when I had a cardiac arrest during what I thought would be routine gall bladder surgery. My blood pressure dropped as my heart stopped. For about three minutes, I entered a "thin place." A "code blue"—the highest acute medical emergency. The anesthesiologist jolted me with CPR and epinephrine to save my life.

When that specialist visited me in recovery, I asked if she would remove her mask so I could see her face and remember her. She smiled as she did. I will never forget her! And then I asked, "You saved my life, didn't you?"

She replied humbly, "I was just doing my job." Just doing her job.

When I eventually saw my family doctor for his follow-up, he walked in and exclaimed, "Roger, you were meant to be here." Then, later he said, "The job of an anesthesiologist is ninety percent boredom and ten percent terror!"

I thank God she knew precisely what to do in that ten percent thin place of terror between life and death. God was with her @ work.

I now buzz with more acute urgency to stockpile my treasures in heaven (see Matthew 6:20). Where do my deep gladness and the world's great hunger meet?

I recall Paul's sermon in Antioch, "For David, after he had served the purpose of God in his own generation, fell asleep and was laid with his fathers" (Acts 13:36). When will I have served God's purpose in my generation and fall asleep? We all have only one bullet. When we fire it, it had better count. Annie Dillard muses, "How we spend our days is, of course, how we spend our lives."[12]

Paul offers us a life-long, presence-centered workplace strategy: "Whatever you do, work heartily, as for the Lord and not for men, knowing that from the Lord you will receive the inheritance as your reward. You are serving the Lord Christ" (Colossians 3:23–24). And remember, God is @ work.

12

Kingdom Come

Presence-Centered Mission and Justice

> We need a new generation of Christians engaged in mission, kingdom vocational living, cultural engagement, and biblical justice—filled with His Spirit, formed by the way of Jesus, and shaped by heavenly wisdom.
>
> Mark Sayers[1]

Gone are the days when the church occupied a prominent place in our communities and culture as cathedrals and churches in town centers once did. We live in a post-Christian culture. Yes, some politicians end their speeches with "God bless America," and some athletes point to heaven after a rip-roaring homer or touchdown, and the odd mention of prayer, the Bible or the Church appear in the public domain. But our culture squeezed Christian faith into the private domain, where it is okay for you personally but not for society publicly. The tirade of secular and liberal voices consigned a Christian voice in the West[2] to the penalty box, disconnected from the game. Like a cacophony of magpies, the blaring voices of pluralism prevail.

Religion is alive and allowed, but not as a privileged and powerful voice anymore. Gordon T. Smith comments in his remarkable book *Wisdom from Babylon*:

> In addition to religious pluralism, there is another dynamic at play: secularization. In many respects, the growth of a secular mindset is the most significant development of the last fifty to sixty years. *Secularity* does not mean no religion; it means rather that religion is privatized, no longer occupying a privileged voice in the public square. It is different from *secularism*—that is, the assumption in the public square that the default response to any issue or concern is a secular one, whether it be political, economic, or ethical.[3]

Secularity marginalizes or excludes religious viewpoints. A Christian nationalism that champions a right-wing political agenda sometimes appears like a narrow, angry and militant tribalism to impose Christian faith on a secularized society. Rampant cultural upheaval foments barb-wired ideology over swan-soft virtue. French writer Voltaire warned, "Truly, whoever can make you believe absurdities can make you commit atrocities."[4] Let's wield humble, winsome, prayerful, non-anxious and faithful presence to engage our culture as salt and light.

Can we wrestle back our sidelined Christian voice in a secularized society through combative politics and conspiracy phobias? Is it possible a bungled theology or a warped spirituality seething with a rugged *my* rights individualism is the antagonistic culprit behind such rancor? We need presence-centered mission. Mark Sayers nails it: "Secularism is the attempt to create a system for human flourishing in which the presence of God is absent."[5]

I led an aging and declining evangelical Lutheran church through a revitalization process. They agonized over how they could be and make disciples, become a revival center and reach Millennials. We discussed how sports and music lessons, recreation and entertainment, consumer living and social media drive most families and how the church sits on the margins. From pale apathy to brute hostility, secularized people are not drawn to lackluster churches.

One woman asked, "How can we compete with our culture?"

I replied, "We can't. But we can offer God's presence, and nothing can compete with it. Millennials want to experience God, authentic community and justice. When God's presence dwells in a church, a cascade of blessings gush in. Word gets out and word of mouth draws interest. God is attractive. Let's pray His presence will become so brilliant in this church that it will entice throngs of Millennials like moths to lightbulbs!" I urged them to pray and discern together and follow Ruth Haley Barton's exceptional book, *Pursuing God's Will Together*. It offers unique biblical practices for church leaders and people who generally lack skills in prayer-full Spirit-led discernment.

The Missional Mandate

Countless churches suffer from mission drift. Their default focus is on internal worship services, maintenance and programs that drift from external mission in the community. Paul Harvey suggested, "We've strayed from being fishers of men, to being keepers of the aquarium."[6] Should not the gathered and scattered Church run on both rails of ministry and mission? Jesus endowed the disciples for Spirit-breathed, presence-centered mission. "'Peace be with you. As the Father has sent me, even so I am sending you.' And when he had said this, he breathed on them and said to them, 'Receive the Holy Spirit'" (John 20:21–22).

I encourage churches to pray "The harvest is plentiful, but the laborers are few; therefore, pray earnestly to the Lord of the harvest to send out laborers into his harvest" (Matthew 9:37–38). Two Greek words are hefty: to *pray earnestly* is *deomai* and means "to beseech or make request;"[7] to *send out* is *ekballō* and means "to cast, drive out, send forth."[8] In Lou Engle's words, let's *Pray! Ekballō!*[9] and beg Jesus to hurl workers into His revival harvest in your community.

Is not our mission as His Spirit-empowered witnesses to proclaim and practice the Gospel and make disciples (see Matthew 28:18–20; Mark 16:15–16; Luke 24:45–49; Acts 1:8)? Is it not to share and show the Gospel, heard and seen, through Kingdom power and presence? When kids jam a key into an electrical outlet, it offers a teachable moment. When people feel God's electric power, they are more open to Gospel proclamation. As secularity dominates the culture, the supernatural must dominate the Church.

At a board retreat where five church leaders met to seek God in listening prayer, one asked for boldness to share his faith. They prayed for him. That Saturday night, as they relaxed in the condo hot tub, they chatted with four women who were also there. The conversation shifted to the fact that they were there to hear Jesus' voice (see John 10:27) and that one experienced instant healing as a confirming sign of his call by Jesus to vocational ministry seven years ago.

Wowed by the stories, the women consented to receive prayer and hear Jesus, too. One leader received a prophetic word that Jesus wanted to heal this woman. Another leader had felt unusual pain in his left shoulder and neck and asked if her pain was located there. She said yes and that it had plagued her for several years. This word of knowledge empowered him to offer a sixty-second healing prayer of command to the muscles and to any constricting evil spirit to loosen its grip. Healed moments later, she lifted her arms, eyes filled with tears, repeating "Oh my goodness, oh my goodness!"

The leader announced, "What Jesus has done for your shoulder He wants to do for your soul. And for all of you!" Another leader discerned these women were not believers and shared the Gospel with them. They said they were Catholics but knew nothing of salvation or of hearing Jesus' voice. This leader pronounced, "Today is the day of salvation." All four women said yes to Jesus that night! These leaders hosted God's presence in the hot tub!

For decades, the missional church conversation grabbed my attention. Len Hjalmarson and I added our voices with our book *Missional Spirituality*. We noticed glaring inattention to the relationship between spirituality and mission, and now to God's manifest presence and mission. Rarely treated are spreading the Gospel with power accompanied by healing and deliverance, divine guidance and miracles. The Gospels and Acts, however, stage these with glaring regularity. Rodney Stark comments, "Eusebius tells us that early Christian missionaries were so empowered by the 'divine Spirit' that 'at the first hearing whole multitudes in a body eagerly embraced in their soul's piety towards the Creator of the universe.'"[10]

I have sought to proclaim and practice the Gospel in evangelism and social service. I have served on a hospital board and volunteered at a cancer agency. I have traveled abroad on mission trips to visit orphanages and prisons and distribute Bibles. I have supported a pro-life society and volunteered with Samaritan's Purse for flood disaster relief. We have opened our home to international students and welcomed others to live with us. I have prayed and voted for government leaders and signed petitions that oppose the redefinition of marriage, assisted suicide and abortion. I have ministered to widows and widowers, helped my unsaved neighbors, prayed for them, shared the Gospel and discipled many. My experiences are unremarkable and probably similar to yours.

Presence-Centered Mission

When God's presence beams through our lives, we become radiant witnesses to unbelievers. Tara Beth Leach makes an exuberant case in her book *Radiant Church*. She calls us to a missional spirituality where Jesus states, "Let your light shine before others, that they may see your good deeds and glorify your Father in heaven" (Matthew 5:16 NIV). We are "sacramental saints" or "glory carriers." And Isaiah prophesied, "Arise, shine, for your light has come, and the glory of the LORD has risen upon you. For behold, darkness shall cover the earth, and thick darkness the peoples; but the LORD will arise upon you, and his glory will be seen upon you" (Isaiah 60:1–2).

When I traveled as a district minister, I would use Enterprise Car Rental and stay at Hampton Inn. I got to know their staff. On two occasions when employees asked me what I did, I explained I was a church consultant. They replied they sensed something different about me. I shared my faith and the Gospel with these seekers.

Notice a presence-centered vision and missional purpose for Church of the City New York, which Jon Tyson leads:

> We're a church community in the middle of New York, with a heart for following the way of Jesus in modern culture. It is our desire to see "the fame and deeds of God renewed and known in our time" (Habakkuk 3:2) by pursuing the *tangible presence* of God, practicing *counter-formation* in the way of Jesus, and living on *sacrificial mission* for the renewal of the city. We believe that integrating these three things—presence, formation, and mission—is at the heart of the ministry of Jesus, and is the unique calling of the church in our time and place in history.[11]

A culture of prayer surges throughout this church.

Kingdom Ministry

Here is a pattern for missional discipleship: "Whoever says he abides in him ought to walk in the same way in which he walked" (1 John 2:6). If we abide in Jesus—practice a presence-centered life—we will walk (live) as He did. How did He live? The Gospels show He lived by Spirit-empowered Kingdom ministry:

> And he went throughout all Galilee, *teaching* in their synagogues and *proclaiming* the gospel of the kingdom and *healing* every disease and every affliction among the people. So his fame spread throughout all Syria, and they brought him all the sick, those afflicted with various diseases and pains, those oppressed by demons, those having seizures, and paralytics, and he healed them."
>
> Matthew 4:23–24, emphasis added

Note the three practices of Gospel Kingdom ministry: teaching, proclaiming and healing. The Kingdom of God—His dominion as King—was the central message of Jesus (see Matthew 4:17; Acts 1:3). He preached and showed His jurisdiction over sin, sickness and Satan through the Spirit's power. "But if it is by the Spirit of God that I cast out demons, then the kingdom of God has come upon you" (Matthew 12:28). And Luke reported, "How God anointed Jesus of Nazareth with the Holy Spirit and with power. He went about doing good and healing all who were oppressed by the devil, for God was with him" (Acts 10:38).

Kingdom ministry is where the Spirit-anointed Church proclaims and practices the Good News (Gospel) of God's dominion over sin, sickness and Satan by preaching, teaching and healing. Jesus came to destroy the devil's work (see 1 John 3:8). Jesus handed us authority (*exousia*) over sickness and Satan for Kingdom ministry (see Matthew 10:1–8; Luke 9:1–2, 35; 10:1–20) and for greater miraculous works (John 14:12–14).

205

Mark reports, "So they [the disciples] went out and proclaimed that people should repent. And they cast out many demons and anointed with oil many who were sick and healed them" (Mark 6:12–13). Consult Ken Blue's *Authority to Heal*, Randy Clark's *The Power to Heal* and Mark Pearson's *Christian Healing*. These contain solid biblical and practical content to integrate healing into Kingdom ministry, which many churches lack.

Let's offer healing prayer for people as we share the Gospel message in our worship services and small groups, hospitals and homes, at work, in coffee shops and at parks. Let's foster demonstrations of God's manifest presence and power. Paul confessed, "And my speech and my message were not in plausible words of wisdom, but in demonstration of the Spirit and of power" (1 Corinthians 2:4). Preaching sound doctrine is not enough. The Gospel of the Kingdom includes the Spirit's power in signs and wonders that bear witness to it (see Hebrews 2:4; Acts 14:3).

I admit there exists a so-called "health and wealth" prosperity Gospel theology that attracts some and repels others, with biblical arguments pro and con. Carefully consider this personal greeting/prayer wish: "Beloved, I pray that you may prosper in all things and be in health, just as your soul prospers" (3 John 2 NKJV). The Greek word for *prosper* is *euodóō* and means "to succeed."[12] Should we pray/wish this text for people to succeed in all things, and for their physical health and spiritual success?

The "cure of souls"—a *theological* practice—defined ancient pastoral practice. But now the "counseling of souls"—a *therapeutic* practice—largely defines current pastoral practice. If we look to Jesus, the Chief Shepherd (pastor), what defined His practice?

James advised the sick to invite church elders to anoint them with oil and pray for their healing. "Is anyone among you sick?

206

Let him call for the elders of the church, and let them pray over him, anointing him with oil in the name of the Lord. And the prayer of faith will save [*sōzō*, heal] the one who is sick, and the Lord will raise him up" (James 5:14–15). All can "pray for one another, that you may be healed" (verse 16). Here are three principles for Kingdom ministry healing prayer:

First, we pray in the authority of the Lord's name, not in our name or style. Only Jesus' name heals people afflicted with sickness and demons (see Acts 3:6; 9:34).

Second, the prayer of faith affects results. It is not a faith formula we use but iron confidence in Jesus' name and authority that heals. It is not enough to believe God can heal but God does heal. He wishes wellness, not sickness. Long before Jesus arrived, Yahweh God announced to Israel, "I will put none of the diseases on you that I put on the Egyptians, for I am the LORD, your healer" (Exodus 15:26). From His merciful character, God does what God is. As our healer, He heals.

A taut connection exists between faith and healing (see Mark 5:34; 6:5–6; 10:52; Luke 7:50; Acts 14:9). Unbelief hinders healing (see Matthew 13:58; Mark 6:5–6). God heals some and not others. Healing can be partial, progressive, permanent or not at all. You may need to pray in stages (see Mark 8:22–26). The "already and not yet" Kingdom dimension places healing as a mystery without a method. Jesus taught, "Healthy people don't need a doctor—sick people do" (Luke 5:31 NLT).

I encouraged a disheartened pastor that a batting average of three hundred in baseball is decent (three hits per ten at-bats). Hitters do not give up if they strike out or fail to hit. He was afraid to pray for healing because he and his church prayed and believed God would heal a young woman of cancer. He did not, and she died. Unbelief crawled in.

As we chatted at Tim Hortons about this, the Lord nudged me to pray for his breakthrough and impartation. I received a word of knowledge that his hands would get hot. They did. He became wide-eyed with wonder as he looked at them. I cheered him to rise up in faith, lay his hands on sick people and pray for healing. We will never enjoy one hundred percent results. Nevertheless, we should pray and not give up (see Luke 18:1).

Third, the prayer of faith will "save" or rather "heal" the sick. Used over one hundred times in the New Testament, the Greek word is *sōzō*. It holds a pregnant idea *to save*—as that which delivers and rescues, heals and restores, whether from sin (through forgiveness, Matthew 1:21), sickness (through healing, Matthew 9:20–22), or Satan (through deliverance, Luke 8:36). Jesus' authority to save from sin matches His authority to save from sickness (see Luke 5:17–26). Satan causes some infirmities (see Luke 13:10–16). As sickness is to the body sin is to the soul. God forgives all our iniquity and heals all our diseases (see Psalm 103:3).

I pray for the sick or injured anywhere anytime. I pray for damaged emotions and disorders. I pray for the power of the Lord to be with me to heal (see Luke 5:17). I sit with people until I sense His presence and pray specifically. When I pray for healing, especially when mountain-sized infirmities such as cancer or paralysis loom, I might have a twinge of doubt. But I gaze past the mountain and peer at Jesus, who looms greater with His authority.

The testimony of Scripture, Church history and my own experience verify regular results do occur. God's Kingdom does not consist in talk or theology but in power (see 1 Corinthians 4:20). I check for signs of God's actions where people might feel heat, tingling, euphoria, peace, release or trembling. I thank God and continue praying. People might weep. Sometimes, however, His actions are undetectable.

Compassion drives healing (see Matthew 14:14), and Matthew cites Isaiah 53:4 (and by extension verse 5) as fulfilled in the Kingdom ministry of Jesus. "That evening they brought to him many who were oppressed by demons, and he cast out the spirits with a word and healed all who were sick. This was to fulfill what was spoken by the prophet Isaiah: 'He took our illnesses and bore our diseases'" (Matthew 8:16–17). Notice, He cast out spirits *with a word*!

It is also clear from the ministry of Jesus and God's character that He is on the side of healing and does not send sickness for our own good, unless in judgment. And notably, He designed the human body to heal itself! Paul also discusses the gifts of the Spirit where they manifest God's presence through miracles and gifts of healings (double plural), to restore people who suffer from various kinds of infirmities (see 1 Corinthians 12:7-10; 29-30; Luke 7:21). God uses both medical and miracle. Too often, though, we rely on medical only. And God frowns upon that. "In the thirty-ninth year of his reign Asa was diseased in his feet, and his disease became severe. Yet even in his disease he did not seek the LORD, but sought help from physicians" (2 Chronicles 16:12).

I invited a colleague to speak at one of our district annual gatherings on "The Rivers of Renewal." On Sunday in our home church, he preached an anointed message from John 7:37–39 about the Spirit's rivers of living water that flow inside those who believe. When he prayed at the end of the service, God's presence gradually appeared like an early morning dawn, shimmering with *kāvôd*. A few minutes in, the associate pastor invited me to aid in prayer for a man in the front row. His eyes darted while he breathed heavily as his arms and legs tremored. As we anointed with oil and prayed, we discerned an evil spirit. We renounced it and prayed for blessing and healing. He calmed down. Months later, he and his wife reported to me he had suffered from years of dark depression but was now no longer on medication, free of depression. Jesus healed and delivered this man after a Sunday worship service.

In November 2019, my daughter, wife and I prayed for a vibrant young couple with four children. Their youngest girl suffered from chronic food allergies with severe reactions to most food groups. Because of these allergies, she dealt with vomiting, hours of screaming and eczema that would break out all over her body. This stymied her size and hair growth. The young mother also suffered from food intolerance, which made her esophagus swell, making it hard to swallow and breathe. During the times of prayer, we helped them renounce many generational sins they traced in their family lines. We prayed laser-focused prayers of healing and blessing. God revealed a covenant with death that had been made, and He sent my daughter mental pictures of a dragon that became chained, followed by a land filled with milk and honey. The family now enjoys all food types without reactions, and the girl's hair grew normally.

On June 29, 2021, our lifelong friend Lorna visited my wife and me. She shared how she suffered from numerous physical infirmities after being widowed in January 2016. These included type 2 diabetes, asthma, diverticulitis, irritable bowel syndrome, loss of her voice and chest infections. As we sat together in our basement suite that evening, I felt a nudge to pray for her healing. We anointed her forehead with oil and prayed for each infirmity. As she sat quietly, she saw in her mind's eye a blue ball of light in her hand and could feel its warmth. We sensed her physical ailments were interconnected to emotional wounds. Within a week, she felt better and regained her voice.

Over several months, the Lord revealed root causes from her childhood that had triggered chronic behaviors as an adult. This began a journey through trauma therapy that culminated in emotional and physical healing. At the time of writing, her diabetes is maintained by slight medication. The irritable bowel syndrome and diverticulitis cause little disruption, and her stomach pain is almost gone. Exactly one year later on June 29, 2022, Lorna visited us again. Overwhelmed with joy, she recounted how God encountered her as His beloved daughter with "whispers of glory."

Let the River Flow

Years ago, I was among an expectant group gathered at a picturesque retreat center in Western Ontario for a Vineyard Canada pastors' conference. At our first luncheon, the late John Wimber, Vineyard International leader and special guest, described an open vision he had from the Lord. Let me summarize what he shared.

He saw a mountain lake with a gentle rain falling into it. The water spilled over a dam and cascaded into a river that flowed into a large plain with thousands of acres of vineyards. Men were working the fields and digging irrigation ditches. He conversed with the Lord about it and concluded the lake was God's blessing He was pouring out into the Church, and the stream was the Church. The irrigation ditches were ministry to the poor, weak, sick, broken and lost.

He understood the Lord to say the blessing could stay in the Church with great meetings and eventually end, or we could let the river flow and direct the blessing into the fields. He got the clear impression of co-laboring with God. And if we do not dig the channels and go out into the fields, revival will not spread. We must place evangelism first.

I believe what comes down must go in and out. The Spirit comes down to bless us, so we would venture out to bless others. The Dead Sea is dead because it has no outlets. Let the river flow. A. B. Simpson taught "All missionary enterprise must have its source in a deeper spiritual life," and "no soul can receive this deep, divine and overflowing life and henceforth live unto himself. It makes the world our parish and irresistibly flows out like water to the deepest places of need."[13]

Before I was to speak on prayer and pursuing God's presence to the national staff of the Billy Graham Evangelistic Association and Samaritan's Purse in Calgary, two leaders had an impact on me with their opening remarks. One of them reported on the floods in Pakistan that occurred in summer 2022 and what Samaritan's Purse was doing. He said the church is magnified during major disasters. The other said when our worship is right, our witness is right. And when another staff couple took me on a tour of the 195,000 square foot ministry warehouse, they pointed to a quote by Franklin Graham that embodies the missional vision: "At Samaritan's Purse we don't run from disasters—we run to them. We go to help people in Jesus' Name."

The mission of the Billy Graham Evangelistic Association is "to proclaim the Gospel of Jesus Christ by every effective means and to equip the church and others to do the same." May the Church be magnified in its right worship and witness as it helps people in their deepest places of need and proclaims the Gospel of Jesus Christ by every effective means, presence-centered.

Social Upheaval

As I view the rampant violence and ruin in our world, I get a sunken feeling. Cable breaking news is usually bad. I see the incendiary mayhem in the United States between Republicans and Democrats, police brutality, fake news and cancel culture. Then add woke culture, critical race theory, QAnon theories, the January 6, 2020, insurrection on the Capitol and the immigration quagmire. The vicious division in the country and in the Church present a tangle of spiritual and social problems that rival the worst human disasters.

Canada faces similar turmoil. It harbors historical tensions between French-speaking Quebec and the rest of the country, an enormous population and political divide between East and West and liberal pluralism. Federal laws allow few restrictions on abortion, medical assistance in dying (euthanasia), and a ban on conversion therapy (treatment that helps a person change their sexuality or gender). Canada reels over the grisly horror of residential schools mandated by the Canadian government between 1831–1996. The Church was also complicit.

The goal was to obliterate Aboriginal children of their culture and assimilate over 150,000 into Canadian culture. The discovery of hundreds of unmarked children's graves is a nightmare.

Presence-Centered Justice and Peace

The topic of justice is understandably popular. God sides with the poor and oppressed. He looks to promote well-being, equality, restoration and fairness for all people. He loves righteousness and justice, the foundation of His throne (see Psalm 33:5; 97:2). The virtue of righteousness adorns and executes God's justice through Jesus the royal Son. "Endow the king with your justice, O God, the royal son with your righteousness. May he judge your people in righteousness, your afflicted ones with justice" (Psalm 72:1–2 NIV).

Justice heads the ethics pack. "He has told you, O man, what is good; and what does the LORD require of you but to do justice, and to love kindness, and to walk humbly with your God?" (Micah 6:8). This verse appears in Washington's Congressional Library reading room. To do justice (*mishpāṭ*) is to treat people fairly. Justice drives presence-centered Gospel mission.

> "The Spirit of the Lord is upon me, because he has anointed me to proclaim good news to the poor. He has sent me to proclaim liberty to the captives and recovering of sight to the blind, to set at liberty those who are oppressed, to proclaim the year of the Lord's favor."
>
> Luke 4:18–19

Most of us will not pioneer campaigns to eradicate poverty, homelessness or human trafficking. But God summons certain people, especially during revival, to alter society. In the United States during the Second Great Awakening, for example, Charles Finney believed the Gospel was meant to save people and salvage society. Between 1815–1861, an interdenominational network called the Benevolent Empire appeared. Formed mostly by wealthy businessmen and middle-class evangelicals, it tackled slavery, alcoholism, women's rights, prison reform, education and other social issues. By 1834, its annual income matched the United States federal government's budget.

Alvin J. Schmidt documents how ordinary Christians accomplished the extraordinary for God. People transformed by Christ became social forces that engineered outstanding achievements in Western civilization. Faith-generated Christians helped form the YMCA and YWCA, hospitals, mental institutions, orphanages, the Red Cross, Braille, colleges and universities, the abolition of slavery in England and the United States, women's rights, the rights of unborn children, labor and social welfare and various gifts of music, literature and art.[14]

Do we prevail against hell's gates and advance God's Kingdom? I can cower at culture as if it is Goliath the giant, and I can doubt what I can do with my five smooth stones. How can I practice justice and reconciliation as Christ's ambassador (see 2 Corinthians 5:18–20) in my minor sphere of influence? Michael Brown offers perspective:

> If you feel like it's your role as a believer to stop the spiritual and moral decline of society, you'll quickly become discouraged and worn out. But if you concentrate on advancing God's kingdom purposes by positively impacting one life at a time, you'll be encouraged and renewed.[15]

My wife was an educational assistant for two decades in public elementary schools. Her gracious and patient approach blessed dozens of special needs and behavior children whose teachers and parents noticed the difference she made. One of our friends served on the board of a school district and several social service organizations, and another served on the city council, both to offer their voices for justice in their community.

One of my former seminary students is a provincial prosecuting attorney with a passion for fair justice in the legal world. God gave an associate pastor friend a burden to alleviate child exploitation. I know a former local pastor who is active in the Peace and Reconciliation Network of the World Evangelical Alliance.[16]

Most local churches can explore ways to minister to single parents, the homeless, widows, new immigrants, women's shelters and public schools as well as offer programs such as *Divorce Care* and *Grief Share*. Eric Swanson and Rick Rusaw suggest, "A volunteer in the community becomes a laborer in the harvest field when he or she combines the good news with good deeds."[17] They conclude, "Good deeds create goodwill, and goodwill is a wonderful platform for good conversations about the good news."[18] And thousands of churches use the Alpha program. It originated at Holy Trinity Brompton, a presence-centered Anglican charismatic church in London where Nicky Gumbel redesigned Alpha in 1990. Its Alpha Film Series and Alpha Youth Series is translated into 112 different languages and is global in its evangelistic impact.[19]

I live in Canada. There is a glaring need to erect bridges between indigenous and non-indigenous Canadians and embrace the *Reconciliation Proclamation*.[20] If you would like to know more about this, consult the Citizens for Public Justice.[21] God calls us to make and maintain peace (see James 3:18; Ephesians 4:3). Peace and God's presence stride together. "Live in peace; and the God of love and peace will be with you" (2 Corinthians 13:11). And good Pietists will promote an irenic or peaceful spirit in religious controversies: "In essentials unity; in non-essentials liberty; in all things charity." Todd Hunter comments:

Self-will and peace are natural enemies. Willfulness wins, and peace loses. This is the case because continually insisting on your way and making sure you get it requires force—a force that

215

often comes in the shape of mistreating others. Peace cannot survive in that kind of environment. To consistently seek peace, we need a new imagination for human interaction.[22]

The word *peace* appears over 330 times in the Bible. It is more than absence of conflict. The Hebrew word for *peace* is *shālôm* and the Greek is *eirēnē*. View peace as the culture of heaven on earth that generates wholeness and well-being, flourishing and order, freedom from strife. As twin rivers, peace and glory flood from God's presence (see Isaiah 66:12; Luke 19:38).

Peace is relational. God's Kingdom transcends steak and wine. It fortifies spiritual, social and emotional health. "For the kingdom of God is not a matter of eating and drinking but of righteousness and peace and joy in the Holy Spirit. . . . So then let us pursue what makes for peace and for mutual upbuilding" (Romans 14:17, 19). Peace is a fruit of the Spirit (see Galatians 5:22). Minds set on the Spirit bring life and peace (see Romans 8:6). If we lack peace, we lack the Spirit.

Let this blow your mind. Jesus prayed to the Father, "The glory that you have given me I have given to them, that they may be one even as we are one" (John 17:22). Jesus discloses that He gave *us* the same glory (*doxa*) God gave *Him*. The perfect tense indicates a permanent reality—we are glory carriers! Jesus transmitted the Father's glory that He had to us so we would be one as He is one with God the Father. Quarrels and discord do not exist between Jesus and the Father, and they should not exist between Christians. God's resplendent presence choreographs oneness and unity in love (see verses 23–24).

Let's respect our differences and avoid lethal rifts "with all humility and gentleness, with patience, bearing with one another in love, eager to maintain the unity of the Spirit in the bond of peace" (Ephesians 4:2–3).

In the summer of 2021, we decided to vinyl our back deck. The project became fraught with problems and delays. Over the weeks, mounting anxiety and frustration rattled my soul. In the middle of October, on the job's last day, the fellow I hired arrived around 2:30 p.m. The weather was becoming cool, and he had a narrow window to complete it. Before he arrived, I prayed for self-composure and that I would host God's presence. As I helped him and we chatted, he casually remarked, "Man, you are peaceful. Not like a lot of guys I work with." Our conversation turned to spiritual matters and my vocation. I was an agent of presence-centered peace for him.

Harmony and holiness lodge together. "Pursue peace with all people, and holiness, without which no one will see the Lord" (Hebrews 12:14 NKJV). Peace exudes a warm and unprovoked humility that overlooks icy insults and avoids heated arguments. What is the tone in your church, your family, your personal life? The battles we incite with others start in our own disordered passions. We wage inner wars with ourselves (see James 4:1). We must practice personal disarmament first to pursue peace with others.

I grew up in Southern California. There is a stark need to erect bridges between blacks and whites and to embrace Martin Luther Jr.'s dream he proclaimed on August 28, 1963, at the Lincoln Memorial in Washington, D.C.:

> Now is the time to lift our nation from the quick sands of racial injustice to the solid rock of brotherhood. Now is the time to make justice a reality for all of God's children. . . . I have a dream that my four little children will one day live in a nation where they will not be judged by the color of their skin but by the content of their character.[23]

Check out the Center for Formation, Justice and Peace.[24]

As presence-centered missionaries, let's "give justice to the weak and the fatherless; maintain the right of the afflicted and the destitute. Rescue the weak and the needy" (Psalm 82:3–4).

Not through political force or social action, the right party or the right legislation alone, but through the way of Jesus. A spiritually formed heart will love well through peace and justice.

May you "seek the Lord and his strength; seek his presence continually" (Psalm 105:4). May His Kingdom come and will be done in your life, home, workplace, church and community as it is in heaven. May you seek, experience and host God's presence.

Conclusion

From Renewal to Revival

> The outpouring of the Spirit affects the reviving of the church, the awakening of the masses, and the movement of uninstructed peoples toward the Christian faith; the revived church, by many or by few, is moved to engage in evangelism, in teaching, and in social action.
>
> J. Edwin Orr[1]

God loves new things, not old things. I doubt He gets excited about thrift shops or used car lots, though they serve positive purposes. He announces, "Behold, I am doing a new thing; now it springs forth, do you not perceive it? I will make a way in the wilderness and rivers in the desert" (Isaiah 43:19). This imagery resonates for those who live in hostile places like Alaska or hot places like Arizona.

God operates this way for Israel and the Church in history and eschatology, in renewal, revival and final restoration. The Hebrew word for new thing (*ḥādāš*) means "that which is original, fresh, new thing."[2] Unless we perceive God's new originals, we can miss ways renewal and revival sprout like desert plants after a summer shower. God judged Israel as hardened skeptics who did not know the time of their visitation of Messiah Jesus (see Luke 19:44).

When God manifests His presence, it is unmistakable to some while unrecognizable to others.

One prayer, one sermon, one conference animated by God's presence can unleash a tsunami of spiritual renewal and new things. In late January 1994, Randy Clark, a burned-out little-known Vineyard pastor in Saint Louis, led a four-day church renewal conference hosted by a thirsty John Arnott, who pastored the Toronto Airport Vineyard.

What began in a modest facility with 120 people spread like wildfire to millions from virtually every denomination and nation on earth. They traveled to the new church warehouse to "catch the fire." Its six-days-per-week meetings persisted for a dozen years, and like a pandemic, the fire transmitted to hundreds of countries and thousands of churches. Tens of thousands professed faith in Christ. Even the economic impact on Toronto hotels, restaurants and taxis accelerated.

As I sat in the second row at one of their conferences, the speaker began his message. Then God's Spirit unexpectedly rushed upon me and clothed me with power. Saul's and Gideon's experiences and Jesus' Pentecost promise offer a biblical framework for me (see 1 Samuel 10:6, 9; Judges 6:34; Luke 24:49). God's manifest presence created a shockwave in me with dramatic effects that lasted for hours. That holy occasion rearranged my dome again with an expansive impact and impartation. Humbled, it reengineered my theology of what a sovereign visitation of God can contain, and it fortified my faith for the impossible.

I spoke there three days later for two midweek evening renewal meetings and witnessed God supercharge over 1,500 faith-filled worshipers nightly. For two hours after my message, I prayed for hundreds. The raw firepower in those meetings in Spirit saturation and healing was astounding. It is now Catch the Fire Church that invites everyone to "encounter God's transforming presence" there.[3]

I am unrattled by the usual controversial mixtures of glory and grit. All renewal and revival movements contain errors and excesses. They are never tidy or rational and require mature *Spirit*-ual leaders who will steward and pastor them well. I identify with others who tell of their life-changing God encounters. People like Charles Finney, D. L. Moody, Craig Keener, Heidi Baker and Francis Chan (not that I rank with these leaders). My passion is to be a spiritual arsonist who ignites fires of renewal to revival.

Present-Tense *Spirit*-uality

God can renew parched Christians and churches whose spiritual landscape resembles the South Dakota badlands. He can revive what one pastor called "comatose churches." Salvation Army renewal leaders Danielle Strickland and Stephen Court declare, "He can saturate you. He can neutralize your natural inclination to act selfishly. He can overflow you with the Holy Spirit. He can accompany you through a boundless life lived in overflow."[4] Like an Acapulco cliff-diver, I invite you to plunge into the boundless waters of the Spirit by audacious faith. God unleashes the rivers of the Spirit in present-tense *Spirit*-uality through the following present-tense verbs that promise an endless overflow of his presence. Pray and live into these verses daily:

> "If you then, who are evil, know how to give good gifts to your children, how much more will the heavenly Father give the Holy Spirit to those who ask [*keep on asking*] him!"
>
> Luke 11:13

"If anyone thirsts [*keeps on thirsting*], let him come [*keep on coming*] to me and drink [*keep on drinking*]. Whoever believes [*keeps on believing*] in me, as the Scripture has said, 'Out of his heart will flow rivers of living water.'" Now this he said about the Spirit, whom those who believed in him were to receive [*keep on receiving*], for as yet the Spirit had not been given.

John 7:37–39

Does he who supplies [*keeps on supplying*] the Spirit to you and works [*keeps on working*] miracles among you do so by works of the law, or by hearing with faith?

Galatians 3:5

Rejoice [*keep on rejoicing*] always, pray [*keep on praying*] without ceasing, give [*keep on giving*] thanks in all circumstances; for this is the will of God in Christ Jesus for you. Do not quench [*keep on not quenching*] the Spirit. Do not despise [*keep on not despising*] prophecies.

1 Thessalonians 5:16–20

Revival Floods

There is stadium-size vision for revival these days, and I am all in. I am no expert, but it is safe to say that revivals are not simply evangelistic campaigns or camp meetings. They are sovereign and surprising visitations of God that infuse spiritual life into believers, awaken unbelievers to that life and transform churches, cities and countries as heaven invades earth. *Revival* means "to live again" or "have new life." *Awakening* is often used synonymously. The closest biblical word is *ḥāyâ*, and means to "quicken, restore to life, revive."[5] "Will you not revive us again, that your people may rejoice in you?" (Psalm 85:6). It occurs when a church or community becomes an epicenter of concentrated God. In Charles Finney's words, "God is one pent-up revival!"[6]

In our rickety, post-pandemic world, let's pray for God to inundate our churches with renewal and our cities and countries with revival through His presence for holiness and healing. Mark Sayers remarks, "A revival is when the presence floods a church, a city, or a country, becoming a powerful force that completely reorients the health of that system."[7] I will offer three accounts where prayer, God's presence and community impact attended revival floods.

1. Jonathan Edwards reports on the revival in Northampton, Massachusetts, 1734–35 where he pastored during the First Great Awakening. Imagine this report about your city:

> Souls did as it were come by flocks to Jesus Christ. . . . This work of God, as it was carried on, and the number of true saints multiplied, soon made a glorious alteration in the town; so that in the spring and summer following, 1735, the town seemed to be full of the presence of God. . . . There were remarkable tokens of God's presence in almost every house. . . . Our public assemblies were then beautiful; the congregation was alive in God's service. . . . Those amongst us that had been formerly converted, were greatly enlivened and renewed with fresh and extraordinary incomes of the Spirit of God.[8]

2. At the turn of the twentieth century, Seth Joshua, an evangelist and early leader in the Welsh Revival of 1904, "felt a danger of the prevailing emphasis upon educational rather than spiritual attainments . . . had it laid upon his heart to pray God to go and take a lad from the coal-mine or the field, even as He took Elisha from the plow, to revive his work."[9] At 7:00 a.m. on Friday, October 27, 1904, he held a prayer meeting with about twenty others and closed the session by praying, "Lord, bend us." In that prayer meeting, God answered Seth's prayer with a 26-year-old former coal-miner and blacksmith named Evan Roberts, who prayed, "Lord, bend me."

Roberts had prayed for thirteen years God would send revival to Wales. For three months in the spring of 1904, God gave him a vision for 100,000 souls. It took only eight months—from October 31, 1904, until June 1905—for those results. The flood of revival began at his home church of Moriah Chapel in Loughor during a prayer meeting he led with seventeen youth. The revival advanced like an unstoppable avalanche without advertising or formal promotion. Roberts taught people to pray, "Send the Holy Spirit now, for Jesus Christ's sake." And God did! Wesley Duewel comments:

> Throughout the country there was an overwhelming sense of the presence of God. It seemed to be universal and inescapable. Not only in churches and prayer meetings, but on the streets, on the trains, in homes, and in taverns people were gripped by the Spirit. Rich and poor, old and young—all were moved by God. . . . Indeed the cloud of God's presence hung low over much of Wales for months. The land was covered by a canopy of prayer, and people everywhere hungered for more of God's presence and power.[10]

J. Edwin Orr notes, "The meetings consisted almost entirely by prayer and praise and were under the direct control of the Spirit of God."[11] The Welsh revival fires spread to Los Angeles and stoked the Pentecostal Azusa Street revival in 1906–09. Eifion Evans describes Evan Roberts, "He was like a particle of radium in our midst. Its fire was consuming and felt abroad as something which took away sleep, cleared the channels of tears, and sped the golden wheels of prayer throughout the area."[12] This quote moves me. May I be like a prayer-packed particle of revival radium!

3. The Island of Lewis is the largest of rocky, windswept islands in the Outer Hebrides off the western coast of Scotland. In 1948 in the village of Barvas, parish minister James Murray

224

MacKay and his church leaders prayed for the Spirit's outpouring upon their sin-afflicted parish. Two sisters in their early eighties, Peggy and Christine Smith, unable to attend services, prayed in their cottage twice per week for months that God would send revival to Barvas. They prayed a single text from 10:00 p.m. until 4:00 a.m.: "I will pour water on the thirsty land, and streams on the dry ground" (Isaiah 44:3).

On the other side of town, seven young men met in a barn to pray for revival three nights per week. They prayed Isaiah 62:6–7 for months, and Psalm 24:3–5 was a text that prompted them to question the condition of their souls. An awareness of God left that barn and swept into the parish with a deep sense of sin, holiness and expectancy.

A Smith sister had a vision of their church crammed with young people and an unknown minister in the pulpit. That vision prompted Reverend MacKay to invite Duncan Campbell, a Scottish evangelist, to come for ten days of meetings in September 1949. Revival broke out in the Parish Barvas church on the first night, and news quickly spread throughout the island. Busloads of people began to arrive. The meetings lasted until two or three in the morning. Revival spread to other Hebrides communities and islands and lasted until 1952. A major wave of revival swept the village of Arnol. God's presence enveloped Duncan Campbell everywhere he went. He became a catalyst. Physical manifestations and prostrations were common. God's presence so dazed and impacted people that some tumbled to the ground as they left prayer meetings. Duncan Campbell reported:

> The awful presence of God brought a wave of conviction of sin that caused even mature Christians to feel their sinfulness, bringing groans of distress and prayers of repentance from the unconverted. Strong men were bowed under the weight of sin and cries for mercy were mingled with shouts of joy from others who passed into life.[13]

Social evils were swept away as by a flood in a night, and in the communities touched by this gracious movement you have men and women living for God, family worship in every home, five or six prayer meetings a week in the parish, the ministers and elders doing their utmost to build up the young men and women in the faith.[14]

My heart pounds from these reports. We cannot work up revival from earth. It can only come down from heaven. Let's blare:

Oh that you would rend the heavens and come down, that the mountains might quake at your presence—as when fire kindles brushwood and the fire causes water to boil—to make your name known to your adversaries, and that the nations might tremble at your presence!

Isaiah 64:1–2

We kindle revival fires only through faith-filled, Spirit-prepared hearts that wrestle in united and earnest boiler-room prayer (see Acts 12:5; James 5:17). We must labor, as mothers in childbirth, with prevailing and travailing prayer (see 1 Kings 18:42). I recommend Wesley L. Duewel, *Mighty Prevailing Prayer*. He will bombard you with biblical motivations and methods in how to experience the power of answered prayer.

As the Hebrides people did, let's appeal, "Will you not revive us again, that your people may rejoice in you? Show us your steadfast love, O LORD, and grant us your salvation. . . . Surely his salvation is near to those who fear him, that glory [*kāvôd*] may dwell in our land" (Psalm 85:6–7, 9). In Lou Engle's words, "Revival is God's arrival."[15]

For revival, multitudes pray 2 Chronicles 7:14: "If my people who are called by my name humble themselves, and pray and seek my face and turn from their wicked ways, then I will hear from heaven and will forgive their sin and heal their land." If you pray this, you pledge to humble yourself, seek God's face (*paneh*)—His presence—and repent. There is no revival without repentance. God promises to forgive your sin and heal (*rapha*) your land. When God revives, He heals. He is the Lord our Healer—*Jehovah Rapha* (see Exodus 15:16).

The word *healing* (*rapha*) in 2 Chronicles 7:14 and across the Old Testament can encompass spiritual, physical and social dimensions. Note the context of verse 13: "When I shut up the heavens so that there is no rain, or command the locust to devour the land, or send pestilence among my people." As you pray, expect God to heal your society of sin and sickness. It is equivalent to experiencing *shalom* (peace)—the culture of heaven on earth.

Here is my valiant prayer for you: "That you may be filled with all the fullness [*plērōma*] of God" (Ephesians 3:19)—with the totality of God's indwelling presence jam-packed into your life. And may you journey on the path of life, where in God's presence there is fullness of joy, and at His right hand, pleasures forevermore (see Psalm 16:11). Let's walk this path of daily renewal and joy to revival, red-hot burning as we pursue God's presence. Selah!

Notes

Introduction From Pagan to Presence

1. Jack Deere, *Why I am Still Surprised by the Power of the Spirit* (Grand Rapids: Zondervan Reflective, 2020), 172.

Chapter 1 The Search That Strengthens

1. Richard Owen Roberts, *Repentance* (Wheaton: Crossway, 2002), 17.

2. Philip Yancey, *Disappointment with God* (Grand Rapids: Zondervan, 1988), 224.

3. "Seek" and "Strength," *Logos Bible Software*, FaithLife, 2000-2022.

4. Mike Pilavachi and Andy Croft, *Everyday Supernatural* (Colorado Springs: David C. Cook, 2016), 37.

5. Adapted from Ken Shigematsu, *Survival Guide for the Soul* (Grand Rapids: Zondervan, 2018), 74.

6. "Paneh," BibleHub.com, 2022, https://biblehub.com/hebrew/6440.htm.

7. Peter Greig, *Dirty Glory* (Colorado Springs: NavPress, 2016), eBook.

8. Henri J. M. Nouwen, *The Way of the Heart* (New York: Ballantine, 1981), 58.

9. Daniel Henderson, *Transforming Prayer* (Minneapolis: Bethany House, 2011), 16.

10. "Kābēd," *Logos Bible Software*, FaithLife, 2000-2022.

11. Marjorie Williams, *The Velveteen Rabbit* (New York: Delacourt Press, 1922).

12. "Emphanisō," *Logos Bible Software*, FaithLife, 2000-2022.

13. Walter Hilton, *Toward a Perfect Love*, trans. David L. Jeffrey (Portland: Multnomah, 1985), 61–62.

Chapter 2 From Eden to Eternity

1. A. W. Tozer, *The Fire of God's Presence*, ed. James L. Snyder (Minneapolis: Bethany House, 2020), 41.

2. Mark Buchanan, *God Walk* (Grand Rapids: Zondervan, 2020), 7.

3. John Walton, *The Lost World of Adam and Eve* (Downers Grove: IVP Academic, 2015), 116.

4. G. K. Beale and Mitchell Kim, *God Dwells Among Us* (Downers Grove: IVP Academic, 2014), 18.

5. "Eden," *Logos Bible Software*, FaithLife, 2000-2022.

6. John Milton, *Paradise Lost* (New York: Penguin Putnam, 2000), 3.

7. Fred A. Hartley, III, *God on Fire* (Fort Washington, PA: CLC Publications, 2012), 82, 133.

8. Eifion Evans, *Revival Comes to Wales* (Bridgen: Evangelical Press of Wales, 1982), 70.

9. Joshua Aaron, "Immanuel (Live at the Tower of David, Jerusalem)," *YouTube.com*, 2016, https://youtu.be/epz3LEHvWuE.

10. Jennifer Eivaz, *Glory Carriers* (Minneapolis: Chosen, 2019).

Chapter 3 The Pursuit of Holiness

1. Johann Arndt, *True Christianity*, trans. Peter Erb (New York: Paulist Press, 1979), 21.

2. J. Scott Duvall and J. Daniel Hays, *God's Relational Presence* (Grand Rapids: Baker Academic, 2019), eBook, 136.

3. Bill Johnson, *Face to Face with God* (Lake Mary: Charisma House, 2015), 9.

4. Andrew Bonar, *The Biography of Robert Murray M'Cheyne* (Grand Rapids: Zondervan, 1950), Kindle, 2802-03.

5. John Wesley, "Upon Our Lord's Sermon on the Mount," Sermon 30, Discourse 10, para. 18, *Christian Classics Ethereal Library*, https://www.ccel.org/w/wesley/sermons/sermons-html/serm-030.html.

6. Elaine A. Heath, *Naked Faith: The Mystical Theology of Phoebe Palmer* (Eugene: Pickwick, 2009), Kindle, 92.

7. "The Thoughts of the Emperor Marcus Aurelius Antoninus," trans. George Long, *WikiSource.org*, 2022, http://en.wikisource.org/wiki/The_Thoughts_Of_The_Emperor_Marcus_Aurelius_Antoninus.

8. John Mark Comer, *Live No Lies* (Colorado Springs: Waterbrook, 2021), 102.

9. Richard F. Lovelace, *Dynamics of Spiritual Life* (Downers Grove: IVP Academic, 1979), 214.

10. "Topos," Ephesians 4:27, *Logos Bible Software*, FaithLife, 2000-2022.

11. "Revival Worksheets," *LifeAction.org*, 2022, https://lifeaction.org/downloads/.

12. Charity Gayle, "Throne Room Song," *YouTube.com*, January 7, 2022, https://youtu.be/Xn5n3JKP3sM.

13. Monastery of Christ in the Desert, "Chapter 7: Humility," *ChristDesert.org*, 2022, https://christdesert.org/rule-of-st-benedict/chapter-7-humility/.

14. Timothy Keller, *Counterfeit Gods* (New York: Penguin Books, 2009), xix, xxiv.

15. "Rîah," Isaiah 11:3, *Logos Bible Software*, FaithLife, 2000-2022.

16. "Eusebeia," *BibleStudyTools.com*, 2022, https://www.biblestudytools.com/lexicons/greek/nas/eusebeia.html.

17. Cited by Dale Brown, *Understanding Pietism*, rev. ed. (Nappanee: Evangel, 1996), 61.

18. Richard Owen Roberts, *Repentance: The First Word of the Gospel* (Wheaton: Crossway Books, 2002), 24.

19. *The Book of Common Prayer: And Administration of the Sacraments and Other Rites and Ceremonies of the Church, According to the Use of the Episcopal Church* (New York: Church Publishing, 2007), 79, *EpiscopalChurch.org*, https://www.episcopalchurch.org/wp-content/uploads/sites/2/2021/02/book-of-common-prayer-2006.pdf.

20. Reginald Heber, "Holy, Holy, Holy! Lord God Almighty!" *Hymnary.org*, 2022, https://hymnary.org/text/holy_holy_holy_lord_god_almighty_early.

Chapter 4 The Discipline of Awareness

1. C. S. Lewis, *Letters to Malcolm* (San Diego: Mariner Books, 2002), 75.

2. Ronald Rolheiser, *The Shattered Lantern*, rev. ed. (New York: Crossroad, 2004), 17, 19, 22, 62.

3. Arthur Conan Doyle, *A Scandal in Bohemia* (Holland, OH: Dreamscape Media, 2017), 6.

4. "Sōbaʿ Simḥâ ʾēt-pāneka," Psalm 16:11, *Logos Bible Software*, FaithLife, 2000-2022.

5. For a detailed discussion of this, see Jim Wilder and Michel Hendricks, *The Other Half of Church: Christian Community, Brain Science, and Overcoming Spiritual Stagnation* (Chicago: Moody, 2020).

6. *Jonathan Edwards on Revival* (Edinburgh: Banner of Truth Trust, 1965), 109–120.

7. Larry Crabb, *The Safest Place on Earth* (Nashville: Word, 1999), 13.

8. Philip Yancey, *Reaching for the Invisible God* (Grand Rapids: Zondervan, 2000), 33.

9. Jean-Pierre DeCaussade, *The Sacrament of the Present Moment*, trans. Kitty Muggeridge (New York: Harper Collins, 1989).

10. Gregory A. Boyd, *Present Perfect* (Grand Rapids: Zondervan, 2010), eBook, 16.

11. Brother Lawrence, *The Practice of the Presence of God* (Pittsburgh: Whitaker House, 1982); Jan Johnson, *Enjoying God's Presence* (Colorado Springs: NavPress, 1996); Ronald Rolheiser, *The Shattered Lantern*, rev. ed. (New York: Crossroad, 2004).

12. Rob Reimer, *River Dwellers* (Franklin: Carpenter's Son, 2015), 94.

13. Elizabeth Barrett Browning, "86. From Aurora Leigh," *Bartleby.com*, 1917, https://www.bartleby.com/236/86.html.

14. Lovelace, *Dynamics of Spiritual Life*, 153.

15. Barbara Brown Taylor, *An Altar in the World* (New York: HarperOne, 2009), 24.

16. Ann Voskamp, *One Thousand Gifts* (Grand Rapids: Zondervan, 2011), ebook, 199.

17. Mary Oliver, *Upstream: Selected Essays* (New York: Penguin, 2016), 8.

18. Adam McHugh, *The Listening Life* (Downers Grove: IVP Books, 2015), 112.

19. Brené Brown, *Atlas of the Heart* (New York: Random House, 2021), eBook, 207–208.

Chapter 5 Spirit-Saturation and Fire

1. Martyn Lloyd-Jones, *Joy Unspeakable* (Wheaton: Harold Shaw, 1984), 85.

2. Bradley Jersak, "Healing Our Image of the Holy Spirit," *BradJersak .com*, June 4, 2021BradJersak.com/12722-2/.

3. For empowered evangelical theology and practice, study Wesley Duewel, *Ablaze for God*, and Rob Reimer, *River Dwellers*.

4. Diana Butler Bass, *Christianity After Religion* (New York: HarperOne, 2012), eBook, 337.

5. R. T. Kendall, *The Presence of God* (Lake Mary: Charisma House, 2017), 89.

6. Gordon Fee, *Paul, the Spirit, and the People of God* (Peabody: Hendrickson, 1996), xiii.

7. George Barna, "What Does it Mean When People Say They Are 'Christian,'" *ArizonaChristian.edu*, August 31, 2021, https://www.arizonachristian .edu/culturalresearchcenter/research/.

8. Brian Zahnd, *When Everything's on Fire* (Downers Grove: IVP, 2021).

9. Bill Johnson, *Hosting the Presence* (Shippensburg: Destiny Image, 2012), 97–98.

10. Scot McKnight, *Open to the Spirit* (New York: Waterbrook, 2018), 16.

11. "Homothumadon," *BibleHub.com*, 2022, https://biblehub.com/greek /3661.html.

12. "About Us, Our Founder," *RevivalPrayerFellowship.com*, 2022, https:// revivalprayerfellowship.com/about-us/.

13. Fred Hartley, III, *God on Fire* (Fort Washington, PA.: CLC), 116.

14. Alan E. Nelson, *Spirituality and Leadership* (Colorado Springs: NavPress, 2002), 56.

15. Nancy Leigh DeMoss, *Brokenness, Surrender, Holiness* (Chicago: Moody, 2008), eBook, 428.

16. Armin Gesswein, *How Can I Be Filled With the Holy Spirit?* (Camp Hill: Christian Publications, 1999), 152.

17. "Lambanō," *BlueLetterBible.org*, 2022, https://www.blueletterbible.org/lexicon/g2983/kjv/tr/0-1/.

Chapter 6 Continual Fire on the Altar

1. Peter Vogt, "Nicholas Ludwig von Zinzendorf," *The Pietist Theologians*, ed. Carter Lindberg (Oxford: Blackwell, 2005), 207.

2. Leviticus 6:13. See John Greenfield and Mark Mirza, *Power from on High* (CTM Publishing, 2017), Kindle, and "Zinzendorf and the Moravians," *Christian History*, no. 1 (1982).

3. "Count Zinzendorf," *TheTravelingTeam.org*, 2015, https://www.thetravelingteam.org/articles/count-zinzendorf-the-moravians-prayer-makes-history.

4. Mark Buchanan, *Your God Is Too Safe* (Sisters: Multnomah, 2001), 223, 220, 227.

5. Richard J. Foster, *Prayer: Finding the Heart's True Home* (HarperSanFrancisco, 1992), 133.

6. Henri Nouwen, ed. Robert A. Jonas, *The Essential Henri Nouwen* (Boulder, Colo,: Shambhala, 2009), 100.

7. Daniel Henderson, *Transforming Prayer* (Minneapolis: Bethany House, 2011), 43.

8. Richard Foster, *Celebration of Discipline* (San Francisco: Harper & Row, 1988), 34.

9. "Proskartereo," Colossians 4:2, *Logos Bible Software*, FaithLife, 2000-2022.

10. "Adialeiptōs," 1 Thessalonians 5:17, *Logos Bible Software*, FaithLife, 2000-2022.

11. D. A. Carson, *Praying with Paul*, 2nd ed. (Grand Rapids: Baker Academic, 1992, 2014), 1.

12. "Qāwâ," Isaiah 40:31, *Logos Bible Software*, FaithLife, 2000-2022.

13. Timothy Keller, *Prayer* (New York: Dutton, 2014), 28.

14. Abraham Heschel, *Man's Quest for God* (New York: Scribner, 1954), 87.

15. Søren Kierkegaard as quoted by Peter Vardy, *An Introduction to Kierkegaard* (Peabody, MA: Hendrickson, 2008), 33.

16. Donald Bloesch, *The Struggle of Prayer* (Colorado Springs: Helmers & Howard, 1988), 132.

17. "Paga," *BibleHub.com*, 2022, https://biblehub.com/hebrew/6293.htm.

18. James Goll, *Strike the Mark* (New Kensington: Whitaker House, 2019).

19. David M. McIntyre, *The Hidden Life of Prayer* (Geanies House, UK: Christian Focus, 2010), eBook, 98.

20. Henri J. M. Nouwen, "In Prayer We Present Our Thoughts to God," *HenriNouwen.org*, April 23, 2022, https://henrinouwen.org/meditation/in-prayer-we-present-our-thoughts-to-god/.

21. Frank C. Laubach, *Letters by a Modern Mystic* (London: SPCK, 2011), 8.

22. Dallas Willard, *Hearing God* (Downers Grove: IVP, 2012), 237.

23. Mark Batterson, *Draw the Circle* (Grand Rapids: Zondervan, 2012), 20.

24. John Piper, "How to Pray for a Desolate Church," *DesiringGod.org*, January 5, 1992, https://www.desiringgod.org/messages/how-to-pray-for -a-desolate-church.

25. Andrew Murray, *The Prayer Life* (Chicago: Moody, n.d), 46.

26. Stanley Jaki, *Praying the Psalms: A Commentary* (Grand Rapids: Eerdmans, 2001), 27.

27. "Psalm 138 The Psalm Project," *YouTube.com*, January 19, 2011, https://www.youtube.com/watch?v=URlxQO6uqVo.

28. Buchanan, *Your God is Too Safe*, 235.

Chapter 7 The Burning Heart

1. Kate Shellnutt, "2020's Most-Read Bible Verse: 'Do not Fear,'" *Christianity Today*, December 3, 2020, https://www.christianitytoday.com/news/2020 /december/most-popular-verse-youversion-app-bible-gateway-fear-covid .html.

2. While this book provides a unique perspective, I disagree with parts of his teaching.

3. Bradley Jersak, *A More Christlike Word* (New Kensington: Whitaker House, 2021), 65.

4. Richard Sibbes, *Light from Heaven* (Mulberry, Ind.: Sovereign Grace Publishers, 1995), 57.

5. T. F. Torrance, *Karl Barth: Biblical and Theological Theologian* (Edinburgh: T&T Clark, 1990), 117–118.

6. Bill Johnson, *The Supernatural Power of a Transformed Mind* (Shippensburg, Pa.: Destiny Image, 2014), Kindle, 104.

7. "Hâgâh," *BlueLetterBible.org*, 2022, https://www.blueletterbible.org /lexicon/h1897/kjv/wlc/0-1/.

8. Gordon Fee, and Douglas Stuart, *How to Read the Bible Book by Book* (Grand Rapids: Zondervan, 2002).

9. Bible Project: https://bibleproject.com.

10. Quoted by Max McLean and Warren Bird, *Unleashing the Word* (Grand Rapids: Zondervan, 2009), 27.

11. Charles Spurgeon, "Paul—His Cloak and His Books, No. 542," *Spurgeon Gems.org*, November 29, 1863, https://www.spurgeongems.org/sermon /chs542.pdf.

12. Roger Helland, *The Devout Life* (Eugene: Wipf & Stock, 2017), 69–84.

13. "Millennials and the Bible," *Barna.com*, October 21, 2014, https:// www.barna.com/research/millennials-and-the-bible-3-surprising-insights/; and "Millennials: Bible Readers or Bible-Admirers," *DiscipleshipResearch .com*, February 2017, https://discipleshipresearch.com/2017/02/millennials -bible-readers-or-bible-admirers/.

14. John Bengel, "NT Commentary-John Bengel," *PreceptAustin.org*, February 21, 2015, https://www.preceptaustin.org/nt_commentary-john_bengel.

15. Quoted by Roger Helland and Leonard Hjalmarson, *Missional Spirituality* (Downers Grove: IVP, 2011), 39.

16. A. W. Tozer, *That Incredible Christian* (Camp Hill: Wingspread, 2008) eBook, 177, 179.

17. Duncan Campbell, *Revival in the Hebrides* (Krause House, 2015), digital edition, 9.

18. Craig S. Keener, *Spirit Hermeneutics* (Grand Rapids: Eerdmans, 2016), 5.

Chapter 8 Fruitful Union

1. Will Mancini, *Future Church* (Grand Rapids: Baker, 2020), 15.

2. Rob Siltanen, "The Real Story Behind Apple's 'Think Different' Campaign," *Forbes.com*, December 14, 2011, https://www.forbes.com/sites/onmarketing/2011/12/14/the-real-story-behind-apples-think-different-campaign/?sh=11d751d462ab.

3. Walter Isaacson, *Steve Jobs* (New York: Simon & Schuster, 2011), 329–330.

4. Dallas Willard, *The Great Omission* (San Francisco: HarperCollins, 2006), 4–5.

5. Reggie McNeal, *Missional Renaissance* (San Francisco: Jossey-Bass, 2003), 83.

6. William Mancini, *Future Church* (Minneapolis: Baker Books, 2020), 15.

7. Peter Wehner, "The Evangelical Church Is Breaking Apart," *The Atlantic*, October 24, 2021, www.theatlantic.com/ideas/archive/2021/10/evangelical-trump-christians-politics/620469/.

8. Henri J. M. Nouwen, *The Inner Voice of Love* (New York: Doubleday), 94.

9. Todd Hunter, *Christianity Beyond Belief* (Downers Grove: IVP Books), 157–158.

10. Fred Hartley, "From the Upper Room to the Nations," *Prayer Connect*, no. 10 (May/June 2013): 14.

11. "Ekporeuomenō," Matthew 4:4, *Logos Bible Software*, FaithLife, 2000-2022.

12. Richard Foster, *Prayer* (New York: HarperCollins, 1992), 137.

13. Larry Lea, *Could You Not Tarry One Hour?* (Lake Mary: Charisma House, 1987).

14. Neil Cole, "A Message from Strategist, Movement Leader and Author Neil Cole," *StarlingInitiatives.com*, 2022, https://starlinginitiatives.com.

15. Dietrich Bonhoeffer, *The Cost of Discipleship*, rev. ed. (New York: MacMillan, 1963), 69.

16. Dallas Willard, *Renovation of the Heart* (Colorado Spring: NavPress, 2002), 88.

Chapter 9 The Habitation of Kāvôd

1. A. W. Tozer, *Knowledge of the Holy* (San Francisco: Harper & Row, 1961), 6.

2. Will Mancini, *Future Church* (Grand Rapids: Baker, 2020), 22–32.

3. "What People Experience in Churches," *Barna.com*, January 8, 2012, https://www.barna.com/research/what-people-experience-in-churches/.

4. Christian A. Schwarz, *God Is Indestructible* (NCD Media: 2021), Kindle, 2584–2621

5. Schwarz, *God Is Indestructible*, 902–1220.

6. As written by Wesley in his *Journal*, September 8, 1784, *The Works of John Wesley*, vol. 23 (Nashville: Abingdon, 1995), 330–331.

7. J. Scott Duvall and J. Daniel Hays, *God's Relational Presence* (Grand Rapids: Baker Academic, 2019) eBook, 92.

8. Bill Johnson, *Hosting the Presence* (Shippensburg: Destiny Image, 2012), 169–170.

9. Flourishing Congregations Institute, "Discipleship in Canadian Congregations," *FlourishingCongregations.org*, https://www.flourishingcongregations.org/so/f3Nhr7hUk?languageTag=en&cid=cdfa851e-157f-466d-a0ee-dc0c8f178254#/main.

10. Cited by Jonathan Graf, *Restored Power* (Terre Haute: Prayer Shop Publishing, 2016), 34.

11. Ryan Flanigan guest blog for Dan Wilt, "Making 'Sense' of Worship: Scripture, Spirit, and Sacrament," *Danwilt.com*, February 9, 2016, https://www.danwilt.com/making-sense-of-modern-worship-scripture-spirit-and-sacrament/.

12. Gordon T. Smith, *Evangelical, Sacramental, and Pentecostal* (Downers Grove: IVP Academic, 2017), 9–21.

13. Quincy Jones, quoted by Joy T. Bennett, "Michael: The Thrill Is Back," *Ebony*, December 2007, 90.

14. Winkie Pratney, *Revival: Its Principles and Personalities* (Lafayette: Huntington House, 1994), 93, citing Basil Miller, *Charles Finney* (Minneapolis: Bethany House, 1969).

15. Charles Finney, *The Autobiography of Charles G. Finney*, ed. Helen Wessel (Minneapolis: Bethany House, 1977), 73.

16. E. M. Bounds, *Power Through Prayer* (New York: Marshall Brothers, n.d.), 32, 35, 38.

17. Leonard Ravenhill, *Why Revival Tarries* (Minneapolis: Bethany House, 1959), 16.

18. *George Whitefield's Journals* (Edinburgh: Banner of Truth Trust, 1960), 60.

19. Clayton Kraby, "CH Spurgeon on the Holy Spirit," *ReasonableTheology.org*, 2022, https://reasonabletheology.org/ch-spurgeon-on-the-work-of-the-holy-spirit/.

20. Daniel L. Block, *For the Glory of God* (Grand Rapids: Baker Academic, 2014), eBook, 982.

21. Jim Cymbala, *Storm* (Grand Rapids: Zondervan, 2014), 75.

22. "85 Veni Sancte Spiritus - Come Holy Spirit," *ChurchOfEngland.org*, 2022, https://www.churchofengland.org/prayer-and-worship/worship-texts-and-resources/common-worship/daily-prayer/canticles-daily-59.

23. While Baptism is also a sacrament, I have chosen only to deal with the Eucharist in this section.

24. Gordon T. Smith, *A Holy Meal* (Grand Rapids: Baker Academic, 2004), 116.

25. Bill Johnson and Kris Vallotton, *The Supernatural Ways of Royalty* (Shippensburg, Pa.: Destiny Image, 2006), 21.

26. *Frozen II*, directed by Jennifer Lee and Chris Buck (Walt Disney Pictures, 2019).

27. Eugene Peterson (@PetersonDaily), "Waiting in prayer is a disciplined refusal," January 1, 2016, https://twitter.com/petersondaily/status/684195642474905601.

28. Fred Hartley, "From the Upper Room to the Nations," *Prayer Connect*, no. 10 (May/June 2013): 18–19.

29. John Piippo, *Leading the Presence-Driven Church* (Bloomington: Westbow Press, 2018).

30. Ruth Haley Barton, *Strengthening the Soul of Your Leadership* (Downers Grove: IVP Books, 2008), 151.

Chapter 10 Home-Based Bethel

1. "Bethel," *BibleHub.com*, 2022, https://biblehub.com/hebrew/1008.htm.

2. Vidor, King, et al. *The Wizard of Oz*, Metro-Goldwyn-Mayer, 1939.

3. John Newton, "My Profile," *JohnNewton.org*, September 22, 2022, https://www.johnnewton.org/Groups/222560/The_John_Newton/new_menus/About_John_Newton/About_John_Newton.aspx.

4. Bradley Jersak, *Can You Hear Me?* (Abbotsford: Fresh Wind Press, 2012), eBook, 352–360.

5. Regina Brett, *God Never Blinks* (New York: Grand Central, 2010), 170–171.

6. Derek Kidner, *Psalms 73–150*, Tyndale Old Testament Commentaries (Downers Grove: IVP Academic, 1975), Logos.

7. GodTube Staff, "It Is Well With My Soul," *GodTube.com*, 2022, https://www.godtube.com/popular-hymns/it-is-well-with-my-soul/.

8. Gary Smalley and John Trent, *The Blessing* (New York: Pocket Books, 1986).

Chapter 11 God @ Work

1. Neil Cole, *Viral: Hearing God's Voice in a Global Pandemic and Beyond* (Starling Initiatives, 2021), 9.

2. Adapted from Os Hillman, *The 9 to 5 Window* (Ventura: Regal, 2005), 65.

3. The Latin root of vocation, *vocare*, means "voice."

4. Frederick Buechner, "Vocation," *FrederickBuechner.com*, 2022, https://www.frederickbuechner.com/quote-of-the-day/2017/7/18/vocation.

5. Hillman, *The 9 to 5 Window*, 23.

6. Denise Daniels and Shannon Vandewarker, *Working in the Presence of God* (Peabody: Hendrickson, 2019), 17.

7. Daniels and Vandewarker, *Working in the Presence of God*, 17.

8. Hillman, *The 9 to 5 Window*, 13.

9. Faith and Work: https://www.faithandwork.co.

10. Michael Frost and Alan Hirsch, *Shaping of Things to Come* (Grand Rapids: Baker, 2013), 137.

11. David Hansen, *The Art of Pastoring* (Downers Grove: InterVarsity Press, 1994), 11.

12. Annie Dillard, *The Writing Life* (New York: HarperCollins eBooks, 2013), 27.

Chapter 12 Kingdom Come

1. Mark Sayers, *Reappearing Church* (Chicago: Moody, 2019), eBook, 80.

2. Western Europe, the US, Canada, New Zealand, and Australia, whose settlers came from Western Europe.

3. Gordon T. Smith, *Wisdom from Babylon* (Downers Grove: IVP Academic, 2020), 7–8.

4. Walter Olson, "The Origins of a Warning from Voltaire," *Cato.org*, December 20, 2020, https://www.cato.org/publications/commentary/origins -warning-from-voltaire. The more literal version is, "Certainly, anyone who has the power to make you believe absurdities has the power to make you commit injustices," as cited in Norman Lewis Torrey, *Les Philosophes: The Philosophers of the Enlightenment and Modern Democracy* (New York: Capricorn, 1961), 277.

5. Sayers, *ReAppearing Church*, 160.

6. "Fishers of Men? Or Keepers of the Aquarium?" *MessageMissions .com*, May 8, 2014, https://messagemissions.com/fishers-of-men-or-keepers -of-the-aquarium/.

7. "Deomai," *BlueLetterBible,org*, 2022, https://www.blueletterbible.org /lexicon/g1189/kjv/tr/0-1/.

8. "Ekballo," *BlueLetterBible.org*, 2022, https://www.blueletterbible.org /lexicon/g1544/kjv/tr/0-1/.

9. Lou Engle, *Pray! Ekballo!* (Colorado Springs: Lou Engle Ministries, 2019).

10. Rodney Stark, *The Rise of Christianity* (New York: HarperCollins, 1997), 13.

11. Church of the City New York, "Vision and Beliefs," *Church of the City New York*, 2022, https://www.church.nyc/beliefs.

12. *Euodóō*, 3 John 2, *Logos Bible Software*, FaithLife, 2000-2022.

13. A. B. Simpson, "Aggressive Christianity," cited by Kenneth L. Draper in *Readings in Alliance History and Thought* (NP: 2001), 157, n. 33.

14. Alvin J. Schmidt, *How Christianity Changed the World* (Grand Rapids: Zondervan, 2004).

15. Michael Brown (@DrMichaelLBrown), "If you feel like it's your role as a believer to stop the spiritual and moral decline," Twitter, June 7, 2021, https://twitter.com/drmichaellbrown/status/1402107421519138821.

16. Peace and Reconciliation Network: https://www.waybase.com/discover/listings/4c197e68-24a8-49ba-a101-3ac4e2b8678c.

17. Eric Swanson and Rick Rusaw, *The Externally Focused Quest* (San Francisco: Jossey-Bass, 2010), 156.

18. Ibid., 161.

19. Alpha: https://alpha.org/about/.

20. "Indigenous Relations," *EvangelicalFellowship.ca*, 2022, https://www.evangelicalfellowship.ca/IndigenousRelations?details=true#tab2.

21. Citizens for Public Justice: https://cpj.ca.

22. Todd Hunter, Facebook, July 30, 2021.

23. "Read Martin Luther Jr.'s 'I Have a Dream' Speech in its Entirety," *NPR.org*, January 14, 2022, https://www.npr.org/2010/01/18/122701268/i-have-a-dream-speech-in-its-entirety.

24. Center for Formation, Justice and Peace: http://centerfjp.org/.

Conclusion From Renewal to Revival

1. J. Edwin Orr, *The Eager Feet: Evangelical Awakenings 1790–1830* (Chicago: Moody, 1975), 248.

2. "Hādāš," *BlueLetterBible.org*, 2022, https://www.blueletterbible.org/lexicon/h2319/kjv/wlc/0-1/.

3. Catch the Fire Church: https://ctftoronto.com/about.

4. Danielle Strickland and Stephen Court, *Boundless: Living Life in Overflow* (Oxford: Monarch, 2013), 73.

5. *Hāyâ*, Isaiah 85:6, *Logos Bible Software*, FaithLife, 2000-2022.

6. Cited in Leonard Ravenhill, *Why Revival Tarries* (Minneapolis: Bethany House, 2004), 138.

7. Sayers, *Reappearing Church*, 156.

8. *Jonathan Edwards on Revival* (Edinburgh: The Banner of Truth Trust, 1965), 13–15.

9. Eifion Evans, *The Welsh Revival of 1904* (Bridgend: Evangelical Press of Wales, 1969), 63.

10. Wesley Duewel, *Revival Fire* (Grand Rapids: Zondervan, 1995), 132.

11. Orr, *The Eager Feet*, 20.

12. Evans, *The Welsh Revival of 1904*, 72.

13. Brian Edwards, *Revival* (Durham: Evangelical Press, 2004), 116.

14. Duncan Campbell, *Revival in the Hebrides* (Kraus House, 2015), Kindle, 105.

15. Joanne Kwok, "'Ask Largely of God': Lou Engle Rallies the Youth of Singapore to Pray," *Thirst.Sg*, November 25, 2017, https://thirst.sg/ask-largely-god-lou-engle-rallies-youth-singapore-pray/.

Roger Helland (Th.M., Dallas Theological Seminary, DMin., Trinity Western University) is the Prayer Ambassador of the Evangelical Fellowship of Canada. He has served as a pastor in the Vineyard, Mennonite Brethren, and Christian and Missionary Alliance, and as a Baptist General Conference district minister. He is an adjunct professor in several theological schools and the author of seven books, including *The Devout Life*, *Missional Spirituality*, and *Magnificent Surrender*.

He is devoted to prayer and the ministry of the Word, to Scripture and the Spirit, to Kingdom ministry and disciple-making, and to piety and holiness. His passion is to stimulate spiritual and missional renewal in the Church.

Website: https://www.evangelicalfellowship.ca/Resources
/Speakers/EFC-Speakers/Roger-Helland

Facebook: https://www.facebook.com/roger.helland.3

Amazon Author Page: https://www.amazon.com
/Roger-Helland/e/B001KIO4EO

Email: rogerbhelland@gmail.com